CARELESS WHISKERS

A CAT IN THE STACKS MYSTERY

CARELESS WHISKERS

MIRANDA JAMES

WHEELER PUBLISHING
A part of Gale, a Cengage Company

GALE
A Cengage Company

Copyright © 2020 by Dean James.
Wheeler Publishing, a part of Gale, a Cengage Company.

LIBRARY OF CONGRESS CIP DATA ON FILE.
CATALOGUING IN PUBLICATION FOR THIS BOOK
IS AVAILABLE FROM THE LIBRARY OF CONGRESS

ISBN-13: 978-1-4328-8097-2 (softcover alk. paper)

Published in 2020 by arrangement with Berkley, an imprint of Penguin Publishing Group, a division of Penguin Random House, LLC

Printed in the United States of America
2 3 4 5 6   24 23 22 21 20

For my dear friend Leann Sweeney,
for years of friendship and
unfailing support,
with much love and admiration.

ACKNOWLEDGMENTS

My thanks start with my agent of over twenty-five years (and somehow she hasn't aged while I have), the incomparable Nancy Yost. Thanks also to Natanya Wheeler and Sarah E. Younger and everyone at Nancy Yost Literary Inc. for being the best. You cannot know how much I appreciate you all!

Michelle Vega is a dream editor, supportive, creative, and insightful. Her edits are always on point, and I am so thankful for that benign presence (aka Natalee Rosenstein) who first brought us together. The rest of the Berkley team is tops also: Tara O'Connor, Elisha Katz, Brittanie Black, and Jennifer Snyder. Thanks for all the amazing things you do.

My friends continue to be the rocks on which I stand, and I am forever grateful for the amazing friendship and support they give. First, my friends Stan Porter and Don

Herrington, especially for being there to keep me grounded and sane while I finished this book; second, to my dear friends, Patricia Orr and Terry Farmer, simply for being who they are; third, to the amazing women of the Cozy Mystery Share a Palooza group on Facebook: Leann Sweeney, Kay Finch, Peg Cochran, Ellery Adams, Mary Kennedy, MJ Maffini/Victoria Abbott, Molly MacRae, Leslie Budewitz, and Heather Blake Weber.

You couldn't ask for better friends and writers to be in your corner when you need cheering up and cheering on.

Thanks also to my sisters from other mothers, Carolyn Haines and Julie Wray Herman. You are the blessings I never expected, or hoped, to have.

Finally, as always, to the readers who have embraced Charlie, Diesel, and the gang so amazingly. Every book is for you, always and forever, and I hope I never fail to entertain you.

ONE

I stared at my daughter in considerable alarm. I couldn't remember ever seeing her like this, grabbing at her hair and stomping around my office. Suddenly she stopped in front of my desk and glared at me.

"I swear, if I could get my hands on Trevor Percy right this minute," Laura said through gritted teeth, "I'd pull every tooth right out of his head."

"Laura, sweetheart, surely it can't be that bad," I said in what I hoped was a soothing tone. Beside me, Diesel, my Maine Coon cat, chirped in distress. Always sensitive to heightened emotion, he seemed to be growing more agitated along with Laura. "What on earth has this Trevor Percy done to make you so upset?"

The glare did not abate. Nostrils flared as she expelled a harsh breath. "What has he *done*? What has he *done*?" She threw her hands up and started roaming around the room again. "He's gone and ruptured his appendix — that's what he's done, the bloody idiot — and now he's out of commission, stuck in California, where he's bloody useless."

"I think you ought to have a little sympathy for him," I said. "A ruptured appendix is no fun." I tried not to shudder as I recalled my own experience some twenty years ago. "I'm sure your agent can find someone else to take his place."

"You have no idea, Dad." Laura's stormy expression, as she continued with her restless pacing back and forth, worried me. I wasn't sure she had heard me. "This could be an unmitigated disaster. 'When sorrows come, they come not single spies, but in battalions!' "

I recognized the quotation from *Hamlet*. In reply, I offered another line from the same play, 'There is nothing either good or bad but thinking makes it so.' "

Startled, Laura stopped pacing and glared at me. "Do you honestly think I'm imagining all this? Come on, Dad, you know me better than that."

"I understand you're upset," I said, a little tartly. "You've also got Diesel on the verge of a nervous breakdown. You have to stop this ranting and calm down."

Laura looked stricken. Her gaze shifted down toward the cat, as if she were only now aware of his presence in the room. She dropped to her knees and held out her arms. "Come here, sweet boy," she said, her voice low and steady.

Diesel hesitated a moment. She called him again. This time he trotted right into her embrace, and she stroked his head, speaking in a reassuring tone. "I'm sorry, sweet boy. I didn't mean to upset you." He responded with a loud meow.

"I think he forgives you," I said, relieved that the storm seemed to have broken.

Laura remained on her knees for perhaps a minute more, rubbing the cat's head and stroking down his back. Mollifying the cat evidently soothed her as well. When she stood, she appeared composed.

"That's better," I said. "Now, come sit down and discuss this calmly. Hasn't your agent found another guest star for you?"

Laura sank into the chair in front of my desk, and Diesel took up position beside her. He rubbed his head against her jean-clad thigh. "Yes, she has. *That's* the problem."

"Why?" I asked. "Who is it?"

"His name is Luke Lombardi."

I detected an undertone of distaste in the

way she said the name.

"What's so bad about him? Is he a terrible actor?" I asked.

"No." She drew out the syllable. "He's a terrible person, but he's actually quite a good actor." Then she added, almost grudgingly, it seemed, "He was nominated for a Tony a few years ago."

That sounded promising, but I still had no idea what lay behind my daughter's obvious dislike for the actor. "Have you worked with him before?"

Laura nodded. "In a community playhouse production in Connecticut one summer, a couple of years before I moved here. *After* he'd been nominated for the Tony." She snorted. "He worked it into conversations every day."

I could understand her irritation, but I had other concerns about the man. I put it to her bluntly. "Did he harass you?"

"Good Lord, no." She laughed. "I am *so* not his type."

"Is he gay, then?" I asked.

She shook her head. "Oh, no, he's definitely straight. He likes his women dumb and stacked." She glanced down at her chest and giggled. "I have two strikes against me."

"I see," I said wryly. Laura, like her brother, Sean, had graduated near the top of her class in high school, and had done extremely well in college. "What are your objections to having him as guest artist, then?"

The theater department at Athena College put on a spring production every year, and they always tried to find an actor of some reputation to play a leading role, not only as a draw to sell tickets, but also for their students to have the chance to work with a seasoned professional. Laura had the leading female role in the play, and her husband, Frank Salisbury, was directing. Laura had professional experience, having spent several years in Hollywood, with bit parts in television shows, as well as theater productions there and back east. She was not a big name, however.

"He's a gigantic drama queen," Laura said. "He throws fits at the drop of a hat if something isn't to his liking. He tries to cow the director into doing what he wants and doesn't take direction well. He can be a bully. And he drinks."

What a charmer, I thought. I began to understand Laura's concerns over having to work with this man.

"Isn't your agent aware of this man's reputation?" I asked.

"She is," Laura said. "He's one of her

clients, too, however, and she said he needs the work." She made a guttural noise. "I could kill her. She swore up and down that she had a perfect replacement for us, and then she sticks us with Luke."

"I suppose it's too late for her to find someone else," I said.

"The contract is signed, and it would cost a lot to get out of it. On top of all that, there's absolutely no time," Laura said. "Plus, rehearsals with him start next week. You're welcome to come by anytime." She hesitated. "I'd love it if you did, in fact. I know Frank won't mind, and if Luke knows my father is watching, he might behave better."

"If he's as obnoxious as you say, I can't see that my presence will inhibit him," I said.

Diesel uttered a couple of chirps, as if in agreement. Laura patted his head and laughed. "It probably won't," she replied frankly, "but it would make *me* feel better, and it might keep Frank from taking Luke's head off."

"I'll do what I can, then, but I don't know that I'll be able to make every rehearsal."

Laura flashed me a smile full of gratitude.

"When does Lombardi arrive?" I asked.

"He's supposed to be here Saturday morn-

14

ing sometime. He's flying into Memphis on Friday and spending the night there, and Frank is going to pick him up in one of the college vans," Laura said. "There's a big reception for him at the Farrington House Saturday night, where he'll be staying for the duration. The department has reserved their best suite for him and his entourage."

"Entourage?" I said. "That sounds pretty grand."

Laura shrugged. "All it probably means is a couple of people: his personal dresser and whatever unfortunate woman he's got dangling at the moment."

I had to admit to a considerable amount of curiosity about Luke Lombardi. He sounded like he could be a nightmare, but I also had complete faith in my son-in-law to handle the situation. Frank was young, but he had a strong character and was not easily cowed or pushed around. He had to be strong, working as he did with the often histrionic personalities in the theater department.

I expressed these thoughts aloud.

"Yes, you're right, Dad," Laura said. "I know Frank can handle him, but Frank does have a temper, and Luke has a knack for finding your buttons and stomping on them."

15

"I still put my money on Frank," I said, though privately her words caused me a few misgivings. I trusted Laura's judgment about her fellow actor, and I could foresee trouble ahead.

A knock at my office door caught both Laura and me off guard, and we turned to see Melba Gilley, my longtime friend and the administrative assistant to the library director, standing there.

"Is everything all right?" Melba asked, frowning. "I could hear a loud voice when I walked out into the hall a few minutes ago on my way to the lounge for some coffee."

The first floor of the antebellum mansion that housed the archive and rare-book collection, along with my office, also contained the library administrative office, along with a staff lounge and a small kitchen. There were two reception rooms as well. If I left my office door open, as I usually did while working, I could hear sounds from downstairs, and vice versa. I hadn't realized Laura's voice had reached a loud enough volume to attract anyone's attention.

"Sorry." Laura grimaced. "I was ranting to Dad about the guest performer who's coming in for the play, and I didn't know I was so loud."

Melba laughed. "Honey, that's okay.

Wouldn't be the first time I heard somebody up here yelling at your dad." She bent to rub Diesel's head. She spoiled him rotten, and he adored her. "What's wrong with the guest performer that you're getting so riled up for?"

"He's a toad," Laura said. "A total drama queen with an ego the size of Memphis."

"Goodness gracious," Melba said, visibly taken aback by the heat of Laura's tone. "Who the heck is this guy?"

"Luke Lombardi," I said. "I'd never heard of him until today, but Laura worked with him doing summer stock in the Northeast." I glanced at my daughter. "Is that the correct term?"

She nodded.

"Luke Lombardi," Melba said, her expression thoughtful. "I saw him in a play a few years ago on Broadway, when a couple of friends and I spent a week in New York during spring break. As I recall, he was terrific."

"He's got talent," Laura said. "I'm not disputing that."

"As a human being, though," Melba said, "he must leave a lot to be desired if you have that kind of opinion of him."

Laura shrugged. "I'm not president of his fan club — that's for sure. Maybe he's mellowed a little by now. He's been having

17

trouble getting work, I think, so I'm hoping he's learned to rein himself in." She picked up her backpack and purse. "I've blown off enough steam now. Time to go home and see my offspring."

"How is baby Charlie doing?" Melba asked.

"Thriving and crawling all over the place," Laura said. "He's trying to pull himself up to stand now."

"He's nine months old," Melba said. "That's on-target. Just wait till he starts walking. You'll be running all over the place after him."

Laura grinned. "We're doing that already. He crawls fast."

"Give him a hug and a big kiss from me," Melba said, as Laura headed for the door.

"Will do," Laura said. "Bye, Dad, and thanks as always for listening. Bye, Melba and Diesel." Diesel chirped unhappily as he watched Laura leave.

"You'll see her again soon, sweet boy," Melba crooned to the cat.

Diesel responded with more chirps.

"I didn't want to mention it after Laura said what she did about him, but I actually met Luke Lombardi in New York," Melba said.

"Did you tell me that before?" I asked,

surprised.

Melba shook her head. "I don't think I ever did."

"How did you come to meet him?"

"One of the friends I went with, Katrinka Krause, has a nephew in New York. He's an actor, but so far he's only had minor roles," Melba said.

"So he was in this play with Lombardi," I said.

"Yes, he was. That's the main reason Katrinka wanted to go to New York. It was her nephew's first big play on Broadway," Melba said. "He was good, though he wasn't onstage all that much."

"Was Lombardi good?"

Melba nodded. "He was terrific. Anyway, we got to go backstage after the play to visit with Micah, the nephew, and we also met the rest of the cast." She paused. "Lombardi slobbered all over Katrinka. It was embarrassing, and it made Katrinka really uncomfortable. Micah saw it and got mad and threatened to punch Lombardi if he didn't leave Katrinka alone."

"Sounds like a thoroughly unpleasant scene." It didn't take much imagination to envision it.

"It was, and it got worse. Katrinka was trying to calm Micah down, and Lombardi kept blustering, trying to provoke Micah, and finally the stage manager had to intervene. Micah got fired the next day, actually. Lombardi insisted, and the manager caved."

"I'm sorry for Micah's sake," I said, "but good for him for standing up for his aunt."

"His mama raised him right," Melba said. "Katrinka was fit to be tied when she found out Micah lost his job. I swear if she could have got her hands on Luke Lombardi at that moment, she would have slapped him so hard, his neck would have snapped."

Two

I recalled Melba's words late that Saturday afternoon while I was getting ready to attend the reception for Luke Lombardi at the Farrington House. If Laura and Frank hadn't been so involved in the production, I would have made my excuses and stayed home. I had heard nothing about the guest artist to encourage me to think tonight would be pleasant or low-key.

Helen Louise Brady, on the other hand, was looking forward to it. We had known each other since childhood, but our paths diverged after college. She had gone to law school. I married my high school sweetheart and moved to Texas to attend library school. Many years later, after the deaths of my wife and my aunt, I moved back home to Athena, Mississippi, to live in the house my aunt bequeathed to me. In the meantime Helen Louise had abandoned a promising career in law to move to France to study French cuisine. When she returned to Athena, a few years before I did, she opened a French bistro on the town square.

We picked up our friendship when I came back. I did the same with Melba, but while Melba and I remained simply good friends, my relationship with Helen Louise developed into a romantic one. We loved each other and spent as much time as possible together, but we hadn't really talked about marriage yet. Both of us seemed content with our current status.

Diesel and Ramses watched my preparations with disapproval, or so I fancied. Diesel always appeared to sense when I was going out without him, and Ramses, the new addition to the household, followed whatever his big brother did. An orange tabby, Ramses was still a kitten, less than a year old. Though he would never attain Diesel's size, I reckoned he would be a big boy by the time he was two.

Diesel chirped interrogatively, and Ramses meowed.

"No, you can't go with me tonight." I scrutinized my tie in the mirror and gave it a minor adjustment. "There are going to be too many people. Stewart is going to be here with you, and knowing him, you'll get a few treats. Plus, you can play with Dante."

Dante was Stewart's toy poodle, and he loved frisking about after Diesel, who dwarfed him. He and Ramses were more of a size, and they tumbled around and chased each other while Diesel mostly watched. He joined in the games from time to time, but he was larger than the two of them together and sometimes intimidated them.

Satisfied that I had tied my tie properly, I turned to pick up my jacket and slipped it on.

"How do I look?" I faced the cats and stared down at them.

Ramses took that as an invitation to rub against my black trouser leg, and I tried not to flinch. A session with the lint brush would take care of the orange hairs that clung to my leg. Diesel meowed loudly, and I took it for approval.

"Let's go downstairs and see if Stewart and Dante have come down yet." I headed for the door, and Ramses scooted ahead of me. Diesel paced slightly behind him.

Stewart Delacorte and his partner, Haskell Bates, shared an apartment on the third floor of the house. Stewart taught chemistry at Athena, and Haskell was a deputy with the sheriff's office.

By the time I reached the kitchen, Diesel and Ramses had Dante frisking around, barking and enticing them to play. Ramses obliged by batting at the prancing dog, but Diesel sat and regarded them with benign indulgence. Or so I interpreted his expression.

"Sharp-dressed man." Stewart whistled when he spotted me in the doorway. "Looking handsome, Charlie. Black suits you."

"Thank you." Compliments tended to make me uncomfortable, but I knew Stewart meant what he said. "I appreciate you looking after the boys tonight for me. Are you sure that you and Haskell didn't have other plans?"

"Even if we had," Stewart said with a smile, "Haskell still would have had to work tonight, since two of the deputies are out with this bad stomach bug that's going around. Don't worry about it. We'll have a nice, quiet evening here, and you can relax and enjoy yourself at the party."

I grimaced. "I'm not so sure about that." I'd already shared with him Laura's opinion of Luke Lombardi and his capacity for being difficult.

"Don't borrow trouble," Stewart said. "He ought to be in a good mood tonight, being lionized by the dignitaries on hand to feed his ego."

"Maybe so," I said. "Laura mentioned that

the mayor will be there, along with the top administrators at Athena. I don't know that Lombardi will be impressed, however, by our local celebrities."

Stewart laughed. "An award-winning actor not impressed by Athena's finest? Surely, you jest."

I resisted the impulse to roll my eyes at him. Even if Lombardi did behave rudely tonight, the mayor and the others wouldn't fail to support the production at Athena. After all, the college would be here long after Lombardi left town. We could all put up with the man's antics for the sake of the school.

Or so I hoped. I had a short fuse on occasions, particularly when confronted by a person behaving badly. That short fuse had caused problems for me a few times, and I vowed to keep those incidents in mind tonight. I would keep my cool.

Helen Louise greeted me with a distracted frown when she opened the door. I stepped into the hall and waited until she closed the door behind me to speak. "What's wrong, love?"

Her face cleared. "Nothing, really." She kissed me, and I slipped my arms around her. She laid her head on my shoulder.

"Something's bothering you," I said

gently. "What is it?"

Helen Louise sighed and disengaged herself from my arms. Her face still close to mine, she grimaced. "It's Henry. I think he's had another offer, this time from a place in Memphis."

Henry was her manager at the bistro. Thanks to his work ethic and capabilities, she had been able to step back from some of her responsibilities and take more time away from the business. If Henry left for another position, she would be back working long hours every day.

"You don't know for sure?" I asked.

Helen Louise shook her head. "No, but I saw a message that one of the girls had jotted down for him in the office. I didn't mean to read it, but I recognized the name of the restaurant. It's one of the top spots in Memphis."

She turned and headed into her kitchen. I spotted a bottle of wine and two glasses on the table. One glass held a few sips of red wine; the other was empty. Helen Louise refilled the one and poured into the other. I accepted the glass, and we sat across from each other.

"Have you asked Henry about this?" I said after a sip of the wine.

"No, not yet." Helen Louise sighed. "I

don't want him to know that I know he's been in touch with that restaurant. I hate the thought of losing him, but I also don't want to stand in his way. He deserves the opportunity to move on to bigger and better things."

"He owes so much to you, though," I said. "You've taught him a lot."

"I have." Helen Louise stared into her wineglass. "If he wants to leave, though, I don't have much choice."

"Do you think it's money?"

Helen Louise shrugged. "Possibly. I pay him well, but he could make more at a place that is so trendy and does a tremendous business."

"Have you considered offering him a partnership in the bistro?" I asked. "That would give him more of a stake in staying here."

"I've thought about that," Helen Louise said. "I'm not sure I'm ready to let anyone else, even Henry, have that much control over my business."

I heard the note of resistance in her voice. She had worked so hard to establish the bistro and invested tremendous energy and vision in it. I understood her reluctance to share it with another person. During all the time she was building her business, however, she'd had no time for a social life, other than church activities on Sundays. That situation had changed, and we had a relationship that was as important to her as it was to me.

For that relationship to grow, we needed to be able to spend more time together. Phone calls late at night, or my eating meals at the bistro while she worked, weren't enough. I had tried hard not to pressure her because I didn't want her to resent me, whatever decision she made. I loved her and wanted what was best for her — and for us.

"I'm sure it will all work out," I said. "Henry has always seemed really happy with the bistro, and I know he has family here."

"True," Helen Louise said. "The situation will resolve itself, one way or another." She stood abruptly and set her wineglass on the table. "Thanks for listening."

I got up from the table. "Anytime, you know that."

She smiled. "One of the reasons I adore you so much. You're always there for me. Let's forget about this and go to that party. I'm curious to meet this guy." She picked up an emerald pashmina and draped it around her shoulders. The green complemented her black sheath dress, and she wore a necklace of chunky green beads the same color as the shawl.

"You look terrific," I said as we headed for the front door.

"So do you."

I chuckled, and she smiled at me.

Moments later we were in my car, headed for the Farrington House on the square. I found one of the few remaining spots in the hotel lot, and we headed for the back entrance.

In the lobby near the elevators, I saw the hotel's catering manager, Donna Evans, looking slightly harassed. I debated stopping to say hello, but I figured she was too busy to chat. Perhaps there would be time later to talk.

Upstairs on the top floor of the hotel, we headed for the palatial suite reserved for important visitors. As we approached the door, which was a bit ajar, we could hear the buzz of conversation. I pushed open the door, and we stepped inside the main living area of the suite.

I spotted Laura and Frank on the far side of the room in conversation with the president of the college. Not far away, several people had clustered around a tall man with a thick mane of golden hair. We stood where we were and observed for a moment. Two of the women with the man were my friends

Miss An'gel and Miss Dickce Ducote. I hadn't talked to either of them in a couple of weeks, and I would enjoy chatting with them tonight. I had expected to see them here. Their family had been part of Athena society since the antebellum days, and they continued the family's long tradition of patronage of the arts. Sadly, they were the last of the family, but both were still going strong despite being octogenarians. They had the energy of persons half their age.

"Shall we go say hello to Laura and Frank?" Helen Louise asked.

"Yes, and after that, I want to talk to Miss An'gel and Miss Dickce," I said. Helen Louise nodded, and we started to make our way through the assembled group. I estimated there were about forty people in the room, and I recognized half of them. I saw the mayor holding court in one corner. Andrea Taylor, the college library director and my boss, formed part of a group of Athena faculty.

Before we made it halfway across the room, however, Miss An'gel spotted us and immediately waved to indicate that we should join her and the others talking to the golden-haired man, whom I had already taken to be Luke Lombardi. Helen Louise had noticed the summons also, and we altered our course to approach the Ducote sisters.

Miss Dickce appeared engrossed in whatever Lombardi had to say, but Miss An'gel looked faintly bored. She welcomed us with a smile, and I gave her a quick peck on the cheek.

"Good evening," she said, her voice low. "Sister and I were looking forward to seeing you tonight. It's been too long. You must come out to Riverhill soon, both of you."

"And Diesel." I grinned. The sisters adored my cat, and he lapped up their attention greedily.

"Naturally," Miss An'gel said with a smile. "Endora and Peanut will be delighted to see him, as will Benjy."

Endora, the Abyssinian cat, and Peanut, the Labradoodle, were rescues the sisters had adopted, along with a young man named Benjy Stephens. He was a rescue, too, I had often thought. Sadly orphaned, with no close family, but the sisters had taken an interest in him, and I thought they had done an excellent thing. Benjy was devoted to them.

The man I took to be Lombardi startled me by suddenly stepping in front of me. I felt Helen Louise take a step back, and Miss An'gel frowned.

31

Lombardi smiled broadly as he gazed at Helen Louise and me. "Good evening," he said in a mellifluous baritone. "Have you met me yet?"

THREE

I had to smother a snicker at Luke Lombardi's way of opening a conversation. Helen Louise and I exchanged swift glances. How puffed up an ego did this guy have? Miss An'gel did not appear at all amused, and I decided Lombardi had used that gambit with her and Miss Dickce. She murmured an excuse and stepped away, leaving us to the actor's dubious charms.

Lombardi chuckled. "That always gets a reaction." He stuck out a hand, and I took it. "I'm Luke Lombardi."

"Charlie Harris," I responded, "and this is my partner, Helen Louise Brady."

"A pleasure to meet you both," he said.

Lombardi released my hand and took Helen Louise's proffered one. He bent over it and kissed it. Helen Louise had lived for a number of years in Paris while she studied French cuisine, and I knew from her expression that she found this present attempt at gallantry as annoying as she had while she was in France.

She reclaimed her hand gently. "Pleased to meet you, too, Mr. Lombardi. We're looking forward to seeing you onstage."

Lombardi beamed. "Then, dear lady, I will do my very best to give a performance that you will never forget." He turned to me. "Mr. Harris, are you a faculty member at the college? Or are you one of the important men in town?" His tone had a mocking edge, or so I fancied.

"I'm the college archivist," I said flatly. "Part-time faculty. My daughter, Laura Salisbury, and my son-in-law, Frank, are in charge of the production. I believe you knew Laura before when she acted with you in summer stock."

"Ah, yes, Laura, *la bellezza incomparabile,*" he said with a lazy smile. "Yes, I had the great pleasure of working with your lovely daughter. I look forward to being onstage with her again. It is hard not to be inspired to one's best performance when gazing upon such beauty."

Helen Louise coughed, and I suspected she had done it to cover a ruder sound. Lombardi was laying it on thick. I had to wonder if this was his real personality or if he was playing a part. The celebrity condescending to the yokels, perhaps? Either way, he was irritating.

"Thank you," I said. "Now, if you'll excuse us, I'd like to talk to my daughter and son-in-law." I nodded, and Helen Louise and I walked away, leaving him standing alone. I resisted the temptation to look back to witness his reaction. I somehow felt certain that he wasn't used to being snubbed like this by yokels like me.

"Well done," Helen Louise whispered as we made our way over to Laura and Frank. "What a pompous ass."

"Laura did warn me that he was full of himself," I murmured back.

"Dad, Helen Louise, I'm so glad to see you." Laura smiled, but I recognized the signs of strain in her expression. "You both look terrific. I love that color on you, Helen Louise."

After I kissed Laura's cheek, Helen Louise slipped an arm around my daughter. "Thank you, honey," she said. "You're stunning tonight, in case no one has mentioned it."

Laura did look particularly lovely, I thought, in an electric blue sheath that accentuated her figure. Her black hair shone whenever the light hit it, and her makeup had been applied so subtly that she looked completely natural.

"Thanks for being here," Frank said after giving Helen Louise a quick kiss on the cheek. His expression suddenly became lofty. *"Have you met me yet?"*

Helen Louise and I couldn't help laughing. Frank's imitation of Luke Lombardi was spot-on.

"Frank, stop it." Laura practically hissed at him. "If he hears you, he'll have another tantrum."

"*Another* tantrum?" I said. "How many has he had since he arrived?"

Frank snorted, and Laura looked aggrieved. "At least two that I know of," Laura said. "Poor Donna Evans had to endure one of them because Luke didn't like the hors d'oeuvres she selected for tonight."

"He'll be lucky she doesn't lace his food with arsenic while he's here," Frank said in an undertone.

"Donna won in the end, however," Laura said, "because she told him she had served what was ordered, and if he wanted something else, he could go out and get it himself."

"That's not like her." I frowned.

"She'd never met Luke before," Laura said wryly. "You don't know how aggravating he can be."

Before we could explore the subject further, we heard the president of Athena College, Forrest Wyatt, calling for everyone's attention. The hubbub died away, and we all turned to face the center of the room, where Lombardi stood beside the president.

"Good evening, everyone," Wyatt said. "Thank you all for joining us here tonight to welcome our celebrated guest to Athena. We are fortunate indeed in having an artist of such high caliber to appear in the theater department's production of *Careless Whispers,* directed by the chair of the department, Frank Salisbury, and costarring his lovely wife, Laura Harris. Luke Lombardi has an outstanding résumé of many fine performances." Here Wyatt rattled off a list of them, concluding with Lombardi's Tony-nominated role a few years ago. I was impressed that Wyatt had committed so much to memory, but that was part of his general charm. The list of accomplishments finally exhausted, Wyatt proceeded with the introduction.

"Ladies and gentleman, our guest, Luke Lombardi." Wyatt stepped aside.

The clapping began, and Lombardi smiled and nodded his head several times to acknowledge the accolade. When the applause ceased, he glanced around the room a couple of times before he spoke.

"I have always heard about Southern hospitality," he said, "and everything I have heard, I have to say, is absolutely true. Thank you all for your gracious welcome to this beautiful town. I can only say to you that I will do my best to live up to your expectations and give you the performance you deserve." He paused for a light round of applause. I had to admit to Helen Louise later that I wondered if that last phrase had a double meaning. "Now, where are Frank and Laura? Oh, there you are. Please join me."

Lombardi waited until Laura and Frank stood on either side of him. Lombardi slipped an arm around Laura's waist, and I noted the slight tightening of her lips. Frank hadn't noticed, from what I could see.

Lombardi continued in the same suave manner. "I worked with this talented and beautiful young woman a few years ago in summer stock, and I had to work hard to keep up with her. You are incredibly lucky to have her here when she could be making a big name for herself in Hollywood or on Broadway."

Despite the fulsomeness of his words, I couldn't help but appreciate the acknowledgment of my daughter's talent. Laura squirmed a bit and looked uncomfortable, and Frank had the traces of a frown as Lombardi went on. "I've not had the pleasure of working with young Frank before, but I've heard great things about him. I fully expect him to push me hard and wring the absolute best out of me for this production. I think you will all be delighted with the results." He paused to offer a slick smile. "Again, thank you all, and let's all return to enjoying the delicious refreshments provided by this lovely hotel."

Applause broke out, more vigorous than before. Helen Louise, her mouth near my ear, said, "He can certainly be charming — you have to give him that."

I nodded. "I wouldn't give him high marks for sincerity, though," I whispered back to her, and she snorted.

"I wouldn't, either," she replied. "I never trust actors anyway."

I knew she didn't include Laura in that general condemnation, and I did not disagree with her. Many actors were fine people, I had no doubt, but Lombardi was not one of them. I trusted Laura's assessment of him, and perhaps my perceptions of him tonight had been overly influenced by that. Still, after meeting him myself, I think I might have come to similar conclusions on my own.

Now that Lombardi had ended his speech, Laura disengaged herself from the arm around her waist, and Frank drew her away after speaking to Lombardi briefly. Spotting me, Laura pulled Frank in my direction.

"Wasn't that completely charming?" Laura's tone dripped with sarcasm.

Helen Louise patted her shoulder. "I have to admire your sangfroid in the face of all that smarminess."

Frank flashed a grin. "What about mine?"

"Yours, too." Helen Louise chuckled.

"Everyone else seemed to lap it up," I said, glancing around the room. Several women, a couple of whom I recognized as faculty from the English department, converged on Lombardi. He was soon enveloped by apparent fans, who appeared enthralled with his pronouncements. I couldn't hear what he was saying to them, but I could see the rapt expressions on their faces.

"I'm hoping they'll never see his other side," Laura said. "He's generally good with the public. It's the cast and crew of the production that he drives crazy."

"Where is his entourage?" I asked.

"They're here," Frank said. "If you look over there by the bar, you'll see his current inamorata, Madame Delphine du Jardin."

40

Helen Louise chortled as we glanced in the direction Frank indicated. "Delphine of the garden? Is that really her name?"

"Who knows?" Laura said.

The lady in question appeared to be upward of forty, perhaps even fifty, with a voluptuous figure tightly contained in red silk with black embroidered fleur-de-lis at the low-cut neck and hem of the short skirt. Her dark hair was pulled back into an elegant chignon with a diamond clip I spotted when she turned her head. She leaned against the bar, sipping from a flute of champagne, while her gaze moved restlessly around the room.

"Does she look French to you?" I asked Helen Louise.

"Possibly," she said. "I'll know if I have a chance to talk to her."

"She claims to be descended from the Bourbon kings of France," Frank told us. "How exactly, I don't know. She rattled names off at me so fast, I couldn't keep track of them."

"Those Bourbons were a fecund lot," Helen Louise murmured. "It's possible."

"Surely she isn't the whole entourage," I said.

Frank shook his head. "If you look a little farther to the right, there in the corner, you'll see Lombardi's dresser, Anton du Jardin."

"Madame's brother?" Helen Louise asked, one eyebrow raised.

Laura grimaced. "No, her ex-husband."

Surprised at this revelation, I regarded the man as openly as I could without appearing rude. Probably the same age as Madame, I decided, but looking far rougher around the edges. His deeply lined face, sallow in the light of the room, gave him a curiously simian appearance. Dark, thick hair and a full beard only enhanced the impression.

"Interesting entourage," I said. "Makes for a happy trio, I'll bet."

"Ever so chummy and lovey-dovey," Frank replied, the irony obvious in his tone. "Three volatile tempers, constant sniping between Luke and Delphine, and frequent whining from Anton. It's a laugh riot." Frank had retrieved the three from their hotel in Memphis this afternoon and driven them to Athena.

"You have my most heartfelt sympathies, both of you," I said, "having to deal with all this."

"Luckily for us it's only for a week," Laura said. "Rehearsals this week, a performance Saturday night, and on Sunday they leave. We can handle it for a week, I hope."

I continued to watch the trio, my gaze switching from one to another in intervals. Their group dynamic fascinated me. I couldn't imagine employing the ex-husband of my mistress, and evidently Anton du Jardin had worked for Lombardi for many years. How many of those years had Delphine du Jardin been Lombardi's mistress? I wondered. Evidently it somehow worked for the three of them, although from Frank's description, they didn't sound particularly happy with one another.

My gaze moved to Lombardi again, and I noticed that one woman, whom I did not recognize, had managed to get him to herself. Her auburn hair shone in the light, and when she turned, I noticed her high cheekbones and catlike green eyes. She was not precisely beautiful, but striking, a woman who would command attention. Lombardi regarded her with a recognizable expression — lust.

Evidently Madame du Jardin also had noticed, because she suddenly pushed away from the bar, champagne flute in hand, and made her way through the crowd to get to Lombardi's side. As I watched, she threw the contents of the flute into his face and slapped him.

FOUR

The flow of chatter in the room suddenly died away, and all eyes turned toward Lombardi and the women on either side of him.

With a dramatic flourish, Lombardi drew a handkerchief from inside his jacket and slowly wiped his face. He uttered a few words in a low voice. Whatever he said set Madame off in what sounded like French.

I turned to Helen Louise and saw a slow grin forming. "French?" I asked.

She nodded. "I haven't heard that type of gutter French in twenty years. Madame has a prodigious vocabulary of invective."

I forbore to ask Helen Louise to translate any of what she heard. The auburn-haired woman appeared not in the least perturbed by Madame's verbal attack. In fact, she seemed to be enjoying it.

Anton, however, took exception to it. He stalked over to his ex-wife, grabbed her arm, and whirled her to face him. Now he cut loose in French, and Helen Louise grinned again. "Oh, the drama," she murmured. "They're well matched, at least in vocabulary."

"Someone needs to stop this," Laura said, sounding thoroughly aggravated. "Maybe we should throw water on them?"

Frank hooted in response.

Lombardi took the stranger's arm and moved her away, leaving the battling couple alone momentarily. The other woman safely out of the way, however, Lombardi returned to the fray. He stepped close to the combatants, dodging wildly flailing arms, and suddenly bellowed, "Silence."

The man possessed a powerful set of lungs. I thought everyone in the room must have started along with me. His command worked on its intended targets, however. Both Madame and Anton ceased bickering at once. Anton turned and stalked back over to the corner he'd previously occupied, while Madame made her way to the bar and asked for more champagne as coolly as if she had not been making a scene only seconds before.

Lombardi faced the crowd and smiled broadly. "The French are a passionate people," he said. "I hope you will forgive Madame and Anton for their display of temperament. We are all somewhat exhausted by travel, and I know they are both most regretful for this disturbance."

A quick glance at Madame, pouring champagne down her throat, did nothing to convince me of her regret. Nor did Anton's glower reassure me.

"I beg of you," Lombardi continued, "to ignore this interruption and to continue to enjoy the fine hospitality of Athena College and this lovely hotel."

A buzz of conversation began to build, and if everyone felt as embarrassed as I did, they would soon start making their excuses and leave. I was ready to go, despite not having tasted any of the food. Helen Louise, however, declined to go when I suggested it.

"You're too easily flustered, my dear." She chuckled. "I witnessed scenes like this every day in France. People blow up and move on. It's better that they get the emotions out instead of letting them build and build."

"Maybe so," I replied, not convinced. "It makes me uncomfortable."

"I know." Helen Louise gave me a quick peck on the cheek. "You're too much a gentleman to be able to enjoy these scenes. But remember that Laura and Frank invited you, and they want your support."

"You're right," I said, chagrined. Southerners, as a rule, didn't care for public misbehavior — my late father referred to it as *showing your ass* — although in private they might discuss the offenders with self-righteous glee. The excoriation of other people's behavior was a favorite pastime, after all. I had no doubt this story would be all over Athena by noon tomorrow, if not sooner. Ticket sales would shoot through the roof, no doubt.

I followed Helen Louise to the buffet table. We both took plates and surveyed the hors d'oeuvres. I zeroed in on the spanakopita, perhaps my favorite, and scooped up four of them. These were enough for me, or so I tried to convince myself. I stepped out of line to wait for Helen Louise. After she had made her selection, we went to the bar, where Madame du Jardin stood contemplating the contents of her nearly empty glass.

"Bonsoir, Madame." Helen Louise followed this greeting with a spate of French too fast for me to attempt to follow, so I munched on spanakopita and let her converse with the Frenchwoman.

Madame's dour expression lightened, and she answered Helen Louise with a flow of words that sounded distinctly different from her earlier use of the language. Helen Louise laughed, and they chatted a bit more before Helen Louise turned to me and, in English, introduced me.

"A pleasure to meet you, Madame," I said. "I regret my French is not good enough to converse with you in your own language."

She smiled. "It is nothing, M'sieu' 'Arris. Your so beautiful Helène Louise has explained to me." Her French pronunciation of my name and of Helen Louise's was charming.

"I hope you will enjoy your stay here in our city," I said.

Madame shrugged. "No doubt I shall, but I will spend much of my time in the 'otel so that I do not have to see that *connard* more than is *nécessaire*. You understand me, I think." She sighed. "That a man with such gifts should be *un fils de pute,* it is *incroyable, oui?*"

I couldn't remember the meaning of the slang word *connard,* but I got the gist of what she meant. "*Mais oui,* Madame," I said politely. Yes, Luke Lombardi did behave like a bastard, I thought, and the fact that he was a talented actor didn't excuse him in the least.

While Helen Louise resumed the conversation in French — which I was more than happy for her to do because she rarely got the chance these days — I glanced toward

48

the corner where Anton lurked. I was surprised, however, to see that he had moved on. I surveyed the room but couldn't find him. Perhaps he had retired to his room after the confrontation.

I watched Frank and Laura chatting with the college president, and they appeared tense as they listened. The man of the hour stood near them, again encircled by a bevy of admirers, including a couple of men. The attractive auburn-haired woman seemed to have left the party. I couldn't find her anywhere in the room. Perhaps she thought that her absence would ease the tension. Madame certainly hadn't cared for the attention Lombardi paid to Mademoiselle X.

After a brief tune in to Helen Louise's conversation with Madame, I tuned out again. I would never be able to follow such rapid-fire dialogue in another language. Once upon a time, I could converse reasonably well in Spanish, a useful skill when I managed a branch library in Houston, but not one I was called upon to use here in Athena.

I decided that Helen Louise would be fine on her own with Madame du Jardin, and I wandered in the direction of Laura and Frank. President Wyatt left them as I approached, offering me a brief nod of recognition, and I joined my children and studied their faces. Laura's strained expression concerned me. Frank had his poker face on, and I knew that meant he was disturbed about something.

"What's wrong?" I asked.

Laura offered a wan smile. "Dad, you always know. What do you think?"

"President Wyatt was expressing his concerns over the production," Frank said, his tone belying the relative mildness of his words.

"In other words, he wasn't impressed with the little scene enacted here," I said.

"No, he wasn't." Laura grimaced. "You know how fastidious he is about everything. Have you ever seen the man sweat? I know I never have."

Frank cast an amused glance at his wife. "Now, honey, it's not that bad. Yet." He drew a deep breath. "We did our best to explain that well-known actors are bound to attract attention and that we can't do much to control their behavior. The college is paying for his expenses here, but not those of Madame and her former husband."

"We are not responsible for those two," Laura said. "No way, nohow. Honestly, Dad, we'll be able to handle this, I'm sure. I don't believe Madame will grace us with her presence during rehearsals, so she won't be around to watch Luke flirting with anyone."

"Speaking of his flirting," I said, "do you know who that woman was? The one with auburn hair?"

"The woman who got Madame riled up?" Frank grinned. "I don't know her, though she looks vaguely familiar. What about you, honey?"

Laura shook her head. "Same here. I think I've seen her on campus, but I don't know her name." She shot me a mischievous glance. "Describe her to Melba, and I'm sure she'll know who this femme fatale is."

I had to laugh at that. Melba had an extensive acquaintance in town. It was impossible for her to know every single person, but she often surprised me by the number of people in Athena she did know.

"Frankly, I'm surprised she isn't here tonight," I said. "I thought she would have wangled an invitation somehow."

"I did invite her," Laura said, "but she turned it down. Told me she had another engagement that she couldn't break."

"That's interesting," I said. "She didn't say anything to me about it." I shrugged. "Not that she tells me everything, of course, especially if she has a new man she's inter-

51

ested in."

"I hope she does have someone new," Laura said, "especially after that dentist she was dating around the holidays turned out to be such a dud."

I remembered the man with a certain amount of distaste. "Melba has never really had good luck with men," I said. "Such a shame, too, because she's a wonderful person. I don't know what it is."

"What are you talking about?" Helen Louise appeared by my side. "What is it you don't know?"

"Why Melba has such bad luck with men," Laura said.

"How on earth did you get onto that subject?" Helen Louise frowned.

I hastily explained the thread of conversation, and Helen Louise's expression lightened. "I see. I think Melba's love life is a subject you'd best drop. She wouldn't appreciate it if she knew you were discussing it."

"I agree," Frank said, with a darkling look at his wife and at me.

"Point taken," I said, not offended in the least. "Did you recognize the woman talking to Lombardi when Madame du Jardin tossed her champagne in his face?" I addressed this to Helen Louise.

She shook her head. "I think I've seen her about town, but I don't know her, so I guess you'll have to ask Melba after all." She grinned.

Frank began to talk about some of the technical issues involved in staging the play, and Laura contributed a few remarks. Helen Louise and I listened with interest, and I was thankful that my son-in-law had changed the subject. We were engrossed in the conversation when the sudden cessation of sound elsewhere in the room became apparent. Our talk stopped abruptly as we all searched the space to find the reason for the silence.

A tall young man, dressed in the uniform worn by the catering staff, stood in front of Luke Lombardi. Madame du Jardin and Anton hovered behind the actor. Lombardi, his expression one of outraged hauteur, regarded the waiter, who held a tray with a single plate on it. I glanced at the contents of the plate and, for a moment, was certain I was imagining what I saw.

No, I decided as I continued to gaze at the plate, those really were pig ears the young man was offering the actor.

FIVE

I tried to stifle my amusement at the sight
of Luke Lombardi's disgusted expression
when he beheld the dish in front of him.
The gurgle of laughter escaped, louder than
I anticipated, and I saw several heads turn
in my direction. Helen Louise poked me in
the ribs with an elbow. I heard the sup-
pressed mirth in her tone as she whispered,
"Stop it, Charlie. You'll have us all giggling."

My laughter had ignited the room, however, because from every direction came
cascades of giggles as everyone in the room
focused on the now rubicund features of
our erstwhile star. Anton du Jardin suddenly
reappeared and thrust himself between his
employer and the tray. With gestures and
sounds reminiscent of a farmhouse goose,
Anton shooed the server away.

His face flushed, the young man retreated
and disappeared into the crowd, clutching
the tray. Slowly the sounds of voices began

to fill the room as everyone resumed their conversations. Anton drew Lombardi to the bar, where they joined Madame du Jardin.

Laura surprised me by suddenly darting away without a word. Helen Louise, Frank, and I looked at one another, puzzled.

"Is Laura unwell?" I asked, concerned. The last time I had seen her behave this way, she was pregnant with baby Charlie.

Frank shook his head. "No, I'm pretty sure she recognized the server as one of her students. He looked familiar. He's not a theater major, or I would have known him."

We three remained together, chatting in desultory fashion, until Laura returned a few minutes later. "Everything all right?" Frank asked.

Laura shrugged. "I'm not quite sure. The server was in one of my classes last fall, and I decided I would ask him how he came to bring those pig ears to Luke."

"What did you find out?" I asked.

"He found them in the dumbwaiter with a note saying they were for Luke," Laura said. "So he brought them to him. He thought someone had sent them up from the kitchen, and he was simply doing his job."

"Strange," I said. "Well, I'm sure Donna will get to the bottom of it."

"Probably," Helen Louise said. "Still, it's an odd thing to happen. I can't imagine anyone serving pig ears at a party like this." Suddenly she snorted with laughter. "I can't imagine serving pig ears, period."

"I believe some people think of them as a delicacy," Frank said with a grin.

"Not I," Helen Louise replied.

"Frank, have you heard from Finn?" Laura spoke abruptly. "I thought he'd be here by now?"

"No, I haven't," Frank said. "Last time I talked to him, about three days ago, he said was coming."

"Who is Finn?" Helen Louise asked.

"Finn Zwake wrote *Careless Whispers,* the play we're doing," Laura replied. "He grew up somewhere in this area but moved to New York some years ago. Still has family here, so he said he'd be in town for rehearsals and the performance."

Frank pulled out his cell phone. "I'll see if he's texted." After examining the phone, he shook his head and put the device back in his pocket.

"I hope he turns up," Laura said. "Although the party really is for Luke, I think Finn deserves some attention."

"Aren't writers usually introverts who don't like being around a lot of people?"

Helen Louise asked.

"Many of them are introverts, I think," Frank said, "but Finn, on the few occasions I've dealt with him, seems to be more out-going."

The playwright's name rang a faint bell, but after mulling it over briefly, I couldn't recall in what context I had heard it. The answer would surface later, I supposed. I couldn't recall a family named Zwake from around Athena. Melba would know, I was sure.

"Why don't you text him?" Laura said to her husband. "It's a shame for him to miss this, and it's an opportunity for him to meet Luke in a more neutral setting than in re-hearsal."

Frank pulled his phone out again and tapped a message. A few seconds later the phone pinged, and Frank glanced at the response. "Says he's almost here." He put his phone away.

"Good," Laura said. "I've only had a few conversations with him, but he seems like a nice young man."

I had to smile. Laura sounded matronly using a phrase like *a nice young man* when she wasn't thirty yet herself. Zwake was probably about her age, if not older, I figured. Helen Louise caught my eye and smiled. I knew she had thought the same thing.

The conversation continued to flow around us, and I was thankful that there hadn't been another scene. The two we'd had were more than enough for my taste. I glanced over to the bar, where Madame du Jardin still stood, but Lombardi had left her and was now once again encircled by a small group of women. Two of them were simpering at the man. I could find no other word that described their expressions more aptly. Lombardi took it all as his due, I supposed. That was judgmental on my part, I realized, and I should have refrained from such thoughts, but something about the man brought it out in me.

Maybe I was turning into a grumpy old man like my late grandfather Harris. An image of him arose in my mind, and I had to suppress a grin. My grandfather had been a crusty old soul, but at heart he was essentially a kind man and a loving father to my dad, his only child. He was all bark and no bite, but I didn't find that out until I was about ten years old.

"Earth to Charlie. Come in, Charlie." Helen Louise spoke directly into my ear, and I started. "Where were you?" she asked. "Is anything wrong?"

"No." I shrugged. "Woolgathering worse than I usually do. Sorry."

I noticed that Laura and Frank had left us. When I glanced around, I saw them making their way to the door of the suite. A tall, lanky young man came through the door and paused to look around. Laura and Frank approached him, and I saw him smile. He had a large, bushy dark red mustache that grew down either side of his mouth to the jawline. The rest of him was clean-shaven. His head sported a fiery red mane of curly hair.

"I haven't seen hair that color in a long time," Helen Louise said. "And that extravagant mustache. You'd never have trouble finding him a crowd."

"No, and he's several inches taller than Frank," I said, "so he must be about six five, wouldn't you say?"

"Yes," Helen Louise agreed.

We had no trouble following their progress through the room toward the area where Lombardi held court. Young Zwake's head stuck out over most of the crowd in the room. They paused when they reached Lombardi. Helen Louise and I began to move in that direction.

We neared them in time to hear Lombardi, Zwake's hand still in his, say, "Delighted to meet the clever writer of such an amusing and entertaining play."

Zwake regarded Lombardi solemnly and extracted his hand. "As long as you don't ham it up, everything will be fine."

Six

I had to admire young Zwake's sangfroid in the face of Lombardi's reaction to the playwright's words. The actor's stunned expression almost made me laugh, but his face darkened rapidly. For a moment I thought he would strike Zwake, but instead he simply clenched his fists, his arms stiff against his body.

"I have never *hammed it up,* as you put it, in my career." Lombardi spit out the words and would have said more, it seemed, but Zwake went on, seemingly unaware of the actor's anger.

"That's good," the playwright said easily. "Your character in the play is a man of intelligence and subtlety, restrained in his emotions, and if you can convey that, you'll be terrific in the part."

Laura and Frank stared at Zwake, and I imagined they were as confused as I was. Zwake appeared to be unaware that he had offended the actor. Was this a deliberate act on his part? Or was he really that blind to the emotions of others?

"Let's get you something to drink, Finn." Laura grasped the playwright's arm and pulled him gently without protest toward the bar. Frank hastily asked Lombardi whether he could get anything for the actor.

Lombardi stared after Laura and the playwright. He turned to Frank and shook his head. "No, thank you. What an odd young man. Do you know him well? Is he always this way?"

"I've met him a few times," Frank said, "but I can't say that I know him more than casually. He has always struck me as a bit remote from the everyday, however."

"I find it difficult, based on this brief encounter, to believe that he wrote this clever play," Lombardi said. "But in my experience, many writers have little personality in the presence of others. They put everything in their work and have little left for social niceties."

"That's an interesting point." Frank caught sight of us and motioned for us to join them. I noticed several women loitering nearby and guessed that they would have been happy to entertain Lombardi, thus relieving Frank of the responsibility.

"I think several of Mr. Lombardi's admirers would like to speak with him." I indicated the nearby women when we reached Frank and the actor. "We've already taken up enough of his time this evening."

"Yes, and it has been such a pleasure," Helen Louise said. "We look forward to seeing the play next weekend. Now, if you will excuse us, we must be going." She held out a hand, and the actor grasped it and bowed over it.

"Dear lady," he said, "anything you wish."

Frank followed us when we left the actor. I glanced back to see the women swarm around Lombardi. Didn't he ever get tired of the attention? I wondered. It would exhaust me pretty quickly.

We paused near the doorway into the hall.

"Are you really leaving?" Frank sounded disappointed.

Helen Louise shot me a mischievous smile. "Charlie has had enough drama for one night." She slipped her arm around mine.

"That's true enough," I said wryly. "Things aren't dull around Lombardi — that's for sure."

Frank heaved a sigh. "I'm hoping this is the biggest drama we'll have during the coming week, but somehow I figure it's only just begun."

Laura hailed us from a few feet away, Zwake trailing close behind her. "You're not leaving already, are you?" she asked. "I wanted you to meet Finn." She gestured toward Helen Louise and me. "Finnegan Zwake, this is my father, Charlie Harris, and his partner, Helen Louise Brady." She finished the introductions while Zwake sipped at his drink, the liquid dark like a soda.

"How do you do?" Zwake stuck out his hand to Helen Louise and then to me.

We both did the polite thing while my mind buzzed over the young man's name. Finnegan Zwake. I knew I'd heard the name before, and I remembered also that the punning reference to James Joyce had struck me as amusing at the time. It couldn't have been this young man's real name; it must have been a pseudonym. But where had I heard it? The name apparently didn't mean anything to Laura, Frank, or Helen Louise. I would run it by Sean and see if he remembered it.

I wanted to ask the playwright his real name, but I realized that would be considered uncouth in the circumstances. I would query Laura and Frank at a more opportune time and find out his background.

They said he had grown up around Athena, so someone would know who he really was.

The playwright's demeanor remained casual and relaxed during the introductions, his expression bland. He did not appear disinterested in us so much as not completely engaged. I wondered what he was drinking and whether alcohol caused his rather flat affect. Perhaps he was always like this.

"We're looking forward to the play," Helen Louise said. "Charlie and I both like suspense, and Frank told us your play is very suspenseful."

"Thank you," Zwake said. "Any worthwhile play must have suspense of some kind. Otherwise no one would sit through more than the first ten minutes to find out what happens next. Same goes for books. If you don't keep wondering what's going to happen, what's the point?"

Zwake sounded only mildly interested in his own views on the subject, but I thought he made good points.

"I agree," I said. "When a writer has created well-rounded characters, readers will be intrigued by them and want to know what's going to happen to them in the story."

Zwake regarded me with a slight spark of

interest. "Exactly." He glanced down at his drink and discovered that it was empty. "Excuse me." He turned and headed for the bar.

We watched him go in silence. Then Helen Louise spoke. "Is he always like this? He's not stoned, is he?"

Laura giggled. "No, not stoned. At least, I don't think so. But we really don't know him that well." She glanced at her husband. Frank shook his head. "I think this is the way he probably always is. Not quite connected to the rest of the world. He's obviously bright, or he couldn't have written this play. But . . ." She shrugged.

"Perhaps he lives too much in his own head to be able to connect completely with anyone else," I said.

"That's a good way to put it," Frank said.

As we watched, Finnegan Zwake had his glass refilled and then wandered over to the nearby wall to examine a painting hung there. He was obviously not interested in returning to resume his conversation with us.

"He hasn't made his reputation yet," Frank said, "but I believe this play ought to get his name out there. With the two leads we have" — he cast a loving glance at Laura — "it should bring the house down. If Luke

66

Lombardi will only behave, that is." He frowned.

"He'd better behave, if he wants to get out of this alive." Laura's tone indicated she would not put up with any shenanigans on Lombardi's part. "I'll wring his neck if he gives us any trouble."

"It won't be your fault if he does behave badly," Helen Louise said.

"Who's behaving badly?" a voice inquired from behind me. I turned to greet Miss An'gel, with Miss Dickce beside her.

I explained to the sisters, and Miss An'gel's expression turned fierce. "I will have a little chat with Mr. Lombardi, I think, and tell him that Sister and I are expecting a good friend of ours from New York who is a noted director there."

"Really?" Laura sounded eager. "Who is it?"

I didn't recognize the name Miss An'gel supplied, but Laura's and Frank's eyes nearly popped out of their heads.

"She's coming *here*?" Frank's voice rose at least half an octave.

"*If* I invited her, she might come." Miss An'gel's wolfish smile delighted me.

Laura and Frank deflated quickly. "You mean you haven't invited her," Laura said.

"No," Miss An'gel replied. "But Lombardi

67

doesn't have to know that." She winked at Laura. "I tell you what. I'll call her and see what her schedule is like, and who knows? Maybe she can come after all."

Laura and Frank perked up again.

"That would be awesome," Frank said.

"I think I should call," Miss Dickce said. "After all, I knew her first." She shot a sideways look at her sister. "Sister's always trying to hog the credit."

"I was the one who thought of it," Miss An'gel pointed out reasonably.

"True," Miss Dickce said. "But I'll call."

"Whoever calls," I said, "I know Frank and Laura will appreciate it tremendously. If she can be here, fine. If not, it will still be a terrific performance."

"I'm sure of it," Miss An'gel said, and her sister nodded her head. "Now, let's go tackle Lombardi. We'll see y'all later." The sisters turned to make their way through the crowd to where the actor stood.

"If Lombardi doesn't behave," Helen Louise said, "I think he'll have Miss An'gel and Miss Dickce to answer to. They'll leave him feeling about three feet tall."

I chuckled. "If it does happen, I'd pay good money to be there to watch it."

"You're still coming to rehearsal on Monday afternoon, aren't you, Dad?" Laura put

68

her hand on my arm.

"Diesel and I will be there, I promise," I told her. Helen Louise and I then bade her and Frank good night and escaped into the hall.

"Are you sure you don't mind leaving the reception now?" I asked.

Helen Louise laughed. "Not much. I wouldn't have minded staying a bit longer to observe Luke Lombardi and his entourage. They certainly aren't dull."

"No, they're not, but they're also not the right kind of entertaining, to me anyway," I said as we approached the elevator. I pressed the button. "What did you think of the playwright?"

"Definitely an odd duck," Helen Louise replied. "That certainly has to be a pseudonym, unless James Joyce titled his novel after someone with that name."

"Yes, I agree. I have heard that name before, but I simply can't remember the context. It will come to me eventually."

The elevator doors opened, and we stepped inside. Thirty seconds later we reached the ground floor and stepped out. "What shall we do now?" I asked.

"Why don't we go back to my house and discuss that?" Helen Louise grinned at me.

"I'm sure we can think of something, don't you?"

"I do believe you're right, Ms. Brady." We headed for the car.

SEVEN

Diesel and I arrived at the office on Monday to find out that Melba had taken the day off. Apparently she thought she was coming down with a cold and decided she had better stay home. I called her at noon to check on her, and her sniffling and coughing attested that she was sick.

"Let me know if there's anything I can do for you," I said. "Diesel sends his best wishes."

Melba sneezed into the phone, and after a moment, she said, "Sorry about that. Give him a kiss for me. Thanks for offering, but I'll be okay. I may be out a few more days. I'm feeling rotten."

I commiserated for a couple minutes, then persuaded her to go back to bed and rest. I shared with Diesel the news that his buddy was sick, and he meowed as if in concern. "She'll be fine in a few days," I assured him. After that, he settled down in the window and went to sleep.

At three o'clock, I closed up the office, and Diesel and I headed for the performing arts center on campus. Rehearsal started at three thirty, and I had promised Laura I would be there.

Today's rehearsal, I knew, would largely be spent on blocking so that all the actors could learn and practice their stage movements. Laura and the student actors had all been through reading rehearsals last week as they worked with Frank, the director, to learn and understand the script. Luke Lombardi was supposed to have read and studied the script in advance, though the fact that he was an almost last-minute replacement might not have allowed him enough time.

After walking in the bright sunlight of the beautiful spring afternoon, I had to allow my eyes to adjust to the dimmed lights in the performing arts center. Once I could see better, I led Diesel to the auditorium, and we walked in.

The auditorium held four hundred fifty seats, and the floor had a gentle slope from the entrance down to the stage. The audience lights were down, but the stage lights were on. As Diesel and I walked down midway to find a seat, I could see the activity onstage clearly.

Laura and Frank stood to one side of the stage, talking. Several students occupied chairs at the back of the stage. The chairs were grouped in a semicircle, and each of the students held a script. I checked my watch. Three fourteen. No sign of Luke Lombardi in the theater yet. I wondered whether he would be on time. I was a stickler for punctuality, and I disliked people who couldn't be on time.

Frank and Laura broke off their conversation. Frank walked over to the assembled cast members. Laura looked out into the house, eyes shaded by a hand, and found me. She waved and called out something to Frank. From my position I could hear the voices, but I couldn't make out what they were saying. I decided I should move closer because they probably wouldn't be projecting to the audience yet.

"Come on, boy," I said to the cat. "We're moving down." I led Diesel down to the fifth row from the stage, and we settled ourselves again. I glanced up to see Laura approaching us.

"Hi, Dad." She knelt facing us in the seat in the row in front of us. She reached over to rub Diesel's head. He occupied a seat rather than sitting or stretching out on the floor. Diesel offered his rumbling purr as a greeting.

"Hello, sweetheart," I said. "How are you feeling?"

Laura grimaced. "Right now, anxious. Hoping that Luke is going to show up on time and behave decently today."

"For everyone's sake, I hope so, too," I said. "I looked him up yesterday and found out that Luke Lombardi isn't his birth name. Did you know that?"

Laura giggled. "Yes, his real name is Elroy Himmelfarb."

"Doesn't have quite the same ring to it as Luke Lombardi," I said.

"No, it doesn't. He had it legally changed when he was in his early twenties," Laura said. "If you want to see him really explode, just call him Elroy."

"I think I'll try to avoid that, unless he provokes me," I said.

"Good," Laura said.

Frank called her to come back to the stage. He waved at me and Diesel before turning back to face his cast. Laura glanced at her watch. "Elroy has three minutes to show up before he's late." She slipped away and rejoined the others onstage.

For a few minutes Frank paced the stage, checking his watch. His expression turned grim, and I knew he was annoyed. Luke

Lombardi was five minutes late, then ten, then fifteen.

At three forty-seven, Lombardi entered the theater and strolled down the aisle toward the stage.

"Good afternoon." His voice boomed in the quiet. "My most sincere apologies. I mislaid my watch. I came as quickly as I could."

Frank's expression didn't change much, but he responded politely, "Very understandable. Now that you're here, we can begin."

When Lombardi joined the others onstage, Frank introduced the student actors. Lombardi made a great show of shaking their hands and beaming at them, offering words of encouragement, telling them all he was looking forward to working with them.

I could see by their expressions that the students found Lombardi charming, perhaps a bit overwhelming. Lombardi was in full star-power mode, and even I felt it. The man knew how to get people to warm to him — that was certain.

Once the introductions had finished, the work began. Frank began with the first scene in the first act, and the play started with Lombardi and Laura onstage. I wondered idly why the playwright wasn't here.

In the fiction I had read involving the theater, the playwright behaved obsessively during all the rehearsals, watching every move, listening to the delivery of every line, not shy about voicing criticism.

Frank spoke to the two leads. "When the curtain comes up, Luke, you will be seated at the desk, tapping on the keys of the computer. Laura, you will be standing at the window, looking out. Luke, you're stage right, and Laura is stage left. Could you assume those positions, please?"

As Lombardi and Laura complied with Frank's direction, I glanced around the theater. I spotted a dark shape two rows behind me, all the way over at the side of the house. As I watched, the shape seated itself, and I was able to make out Finn Zwake in the dim light.

Laura had given me a rundown of the play and its characters. Lombardi played a noted writer, and Laura was his wife. Lombardi had a secretary, played by one of the female students. During the course of the first act, Laura would find out that the secretary was having an affair with her husband and begin to suspect that the two of them were plotting to kill her. Laura's character was an heiress, and Lombardi's character had tired of her, but wanted to keep her money, so a divorce wouldn't work.

The title of the play, *Careless Whispers,* referred to way in which the wife discovered the affair and the plotting. Characters whispered to one another — but audibly enough so that the audience could hear. It was a hackneyed device, but Laura had assured me it was effective. It all depended on the staging, of course.

After half an hour of what was to me frankly tedious stagecraft, I found myself beginning to nod off. Diesel had already gone to sleep beside me. Thus far Lombardi had behaved in gentlemanly fashion, listening to Frank and complying with the directions he received. Laura, I could tell, had relaxed, no longer on edge waiting for Lombardi to misbehave.

I decided it would be okay for me to close my eyes for a few minutes. Hoping I wouldn't snore, I began to doze.

A hand on my arm startled me awake, and it took me a moment to reorient myself. Diesel chirped, and I glanced over to see Finn Zwake occupying the seat beside my cat.

"Sorry," he said in an undertone. "Didn't mean to startle you, but you had started to snore."

I shot a guilty glance toward the stage,

but no one there appeared to have noticed my gaffe.

"Thank you," I said. "I dozed off."

Zwake grinned. "Yes, you did. Can't say I blame you. This is a dull part of the process. Dull but necessary."

The playwright appeared more engaged now than he had been during the reception Saturday night. I supposed that seeing his play in the process of being staged caught his attention, whereas the roomful of people at the party had not.

I took a closer look at the stage. Luke Lombardi was not in sight, nor was Laura. Frank was working with several of the student members of the cast instead. I checked the time and was startled to see that it was nearly a quarter to five. I had dozed for longer than I realized.

"What do you think about how the blocking is going so far?" I asked Zwake, raising my voice slightly.

His expression bemused, Zwake turned to look at me. "Fine so far. I'm just surprised that Luke is behaving so well. Usually he starts kicking up during this stage." He shrugged. "He *always* has thoughts about how things can be done better and doesn't hesitate to let everyone know."

I could have enlightened him by sharing

Miss An'gel's stratagem to ensure Lombardi's good behavior, but I decided that it was not for me to tell him about that. If or when the famous director decided to come down to Mississippi to see the play, Frank could inform Zwake.

I had to applaud Miss An'gel's ingenuity, because so far Lombardi had behaved well. I hoped this would continue because there was enough stress in the whole process of staging a play without unnecessary histrionics.

Zwake and I watched in silence, while Diesel slept between us. Frank continued his work with the student actors, and I began to wonder where Lombardi and Laura were all this time. In their respective dressing rooms, I supposed.

A few minutes later, Laura reappeared onstage, followed in another few minutes by Lombardi. I could tell from the merest glance that Laura was aggravated, and I wondered what Lombardi had done to bring this about.

As soon as Frank finished his current task with the students, he called a ten-minute break and went immediately to Laura. The students disappeared into the wings, leaving husband and wife onstage with the guest artist.

Laura and Frank, heads together, conversed in an undertone, and I couldn't hear anything they said. The tone alerted me to Laura's unhappiness, however, bearing out the expression I'd seen when she walked onstage.

Lombardi waited about five feet away from them, his expression enigmatic. Laura waved a couple of times in his direction, however, and he smirked at that point. I had an uneasy feeling about this. Trouble had begun brewing.

Frank broke off talking to his wife and turned to address Lombardi. "I hear you have problems with some of the staging, Luke. Care to share your thoughts with me?"

I caught the edge to Frank's tone, but Lombardi gave no appearance of having done so. He advanced four steps and regarded Frank with pursed lips.

"Yes, I do have a few problems," Lombardi said. "You have me with my back to the audience far too much. I want the position of the desk changed so that my audience can see me. If they can't see my face, they will lose most of my performance."

Frank stared at Lombardi, and I thought he might explode at this demand to change his staging of the play. Then he nodded. "I see your point. We can shift the position of the desk if you feel that strongly about it."

I could tell that he wasn't happy. He must have had a good reason to have Lombardi face away from the stage, but whatever it was, he evidently decided not to share it with the actor. "Laura will have to shift her position to accommodate it, but I don't think that's a problem." He looked at his wife.

Laura's mutinous expression signaled disagreement, but she gave a curt nod.

Lombardi grinned broadly. "I thought you would see it my way. After my many years onstage, I do know something about stage-craft." His self-satisfied tone annoyed me, and I had no doubt both my daughter and son-in-law felt the same.

"Now, there are a few other things I feel we ought to discuss," Lombardi said. Having won his first point, evidently he felt like pushing his luck even further.

Before Frank could respond to this, a voice from offstage interrupted them.

"Good afternoon, everyone. I trust you won't mind this intrusion." Miss An'gel walked onto the stage behind Lombardi, followed by Miss Dickce.

Lombardi whirled around, obviously startled. I wished I could have seen his face.

Miss An'gel paused in front of the actor. "I trust there are no problems, Mr. Lombardi. That would be such a shame." Her tone dripped honeyed sweetness, but underneath it lay steel.

Lombardi wilted immediately, and I had to stifle a laugh. Miss An'gel was thoroughly in command.

EIGHT

Beside me in the shadows, Finn Zwake chuckled. "I don't know how she's doing it," he whispered, "but I'm loving it. Who is that?" Lombardi continued to grovel onstage.

"Miss An'gel Ducote, and that's her sister, Miss Dickce, with her," I said.

"So those are the legendary Ducote sisters," Zwake murmured. When he continued, his voice became a slow drawl. "I do declare, those ladies are downright amazing. I've been a-hopin' I'd get a chance to meet them."

"They're dear friends of mine," I said. "I'll be happy to introduce you when the occasion permits."

Zwake continued his drawl. "That'd be mighty kind of you, sir. I don't imagine you can get more Old South than these two ladies."

I found him amusing, though I couldn't

exactly say why. He had transformed into someone else. He even held his body differently when he spoke in the slightly exaggerated drawl. If anything, he appeared languorous to the point of going to sleep himself.

Onstage, Lombardi continued to assure Miss An'gel that he was thoroughly happy with everything. After he made a long, rambling discourse on the merits of Frank's directions and Laura's skills as an actress, Miss An'gel cut him off.

"I'm reassured to hear that you're happy, Mr. Lombardi," she said, her voice now evincing more steel and less honey. "Everyone concerned wants this production to be a huge success, and we're counting on you to do your part."

Zwake snickered. "Atta girl," he said in an undertone. "Keep that goose cooking."

Miss An'gel and Miss Dickce made a point of greeting everyone onstage, showing particular interest in Laura, and I trusted that Lombardi registered that. After this, I felt sure he would settle down.

Miss An'gel and Miss Dickce bade everyone farewell and exited the stage. I hoped they would come into the auditorium, but they did not.

Work on the stage resumed, and Lombardi appeared to go along with whatever Frank wanted him to do. I decided that it would be okay for me and Diesel to head home, now that Miss An'gel had laid down the law. I tried not to snicker myself. "I'm sure I'll see you again soon," I said to Zwake, and he nodded, his eyes fixed upon the stage. I didn't press him further for a verbal response. "Come on, Diesel," I said.

My cat sat up and yawned before he stepped down from his seat and followed me placidly up the aisle to the lobby. We emerged into the afternoon sunlight and the coolness of the April day. I had to stand there for a minute to let my eyes adjust to the light after the dimness of the theater. Then we headed back to the library administration building and the parking lot behind it to pick up my car.

As I drove the short distance home with Diesel in the backseat, I thought about Luke Lombardi and Miss An'gel Ducote. As formidable a deterrent as Miss An'gel was, I couldn't ignore the thought that Lombardi might let his temper overcome his better judgment at some point. I hoped to be proved wrong, but we still had most of the week to go until opening night. I also hoped Laura wouldn't be unhappy with me for not staying longer since things appeared to be going well. If she were unhappy, I'd hear about it, I knew.

To my surprise, Azalea Berry, my housekeeper, hadn't left for the day. Diesel and I found her in the kitchen, fussing over the stove and fussing at Ramses.

"Hello, Azalea," I said, shutting the door from the garage behind me. "What has Ramses been up to now?"

Ramses immediately left Azalea's side upon realizing that his big brother — Diesel outweighed the tabby kitten by about thirty pounds — was home. He bumped his head against Diesel's chest, and the Maine Coon chirped in response. I couldn't say that Diesel was precisely fond of Ramses, but he tolerated him really well.

"Oh, he's being his messy little self, driving me about to distraction." Azalea's tone didn't fool me. She adored Ramses, but she tried not to betray it. She had also grown fond of Diesel, whom she addressed as "Mr. Cat," after spurning him for a long time.

"In other words, he's begging for food and following you around, wanting you to pick him up," I said, trying not to grin.

Azalea shot me a look. "I think you oughta start taking this scamp with you, like you do Mr. Cat. I don't have time to be mind-ing no child while I'm trying to get my work done."

I pretended to be shocked. "My goodness, I didn't realize he was causing you so much worry. First thing tomorrow, I'll get him a halter and a leash like the ones Diesel has, and I'll start taking him to work with us. The last thing I want is for you to be upset."

Azalea faced me, hands on hips. "Now, don't you go getting in any hurry. I reckon I can put up with him for a few more days, if he learns to behave himself." She glared at the cat. "Listen to me, Mr. Ramses, you'd best start behaving yourself, or you won't be getting any treats from me. You understand me?"

Ramses, obviously puzzled by the tone of her voice, stared up at her and emitted a sad-sounding meow. Azalea's lips twitched, but she held firm. "Yes, you'd better be good from now on," she said, her voice stern.

Ramses walked over to her and rubbed against her leg. The housekeeper's expression softened. I had to turn away because I didn't want her to see the grin that I couldn't for the life of me suppress. When I first moved back to Athena, into the house my aunt Dottie left me, Azalea informed me that she would be taking care of me and the house, as Aunt Dottie had wished. Frankly, at the time, she intimidated me no end.

As time passed, however, and we got to know each other better — and as she warmed to Diesel and other members of my now-extended family — I was able to see and appreciate the woman for who she was. She could still be intimidating, but at heart she was a caring person. I believed she no longer saw me as a legacy from my aunt, but as a person she cared about and wanted to take care of, the way she had for many years for my beloved aunt.

Her daughter, Kanesha, chief deputy of the Athena County Sheriff's Department, was a harder nut to crack. Kanesha had never completely accepted the fact that her mother preferred to work as a domestic. She made periodic attempts to get Azalea to retire, but Azalea steadfastly refused. When I first moved back, Kanesha was very hostile toward me because I wouldn't fire her mother. If I had even tried to fire Azalea, I knew, she wouldn't have paid the least attention to me.

Over time, and over numerous murder investigations, however, Kanesha and I had come to respect each other. While I wouldn't exactly call her a friend, I knew she was someone I could call on whenever I needed her particular skills. I believed she also knew that about me as well. I hoped I wouldn't have to test her patience anytime soon, though. She could get pretty aggravated with me in some situations. Recently I had goaded a killer into attacking me without having thoroughly assessed the consequences of my actions beforehand. I had vowed to be more careful in the future, and I intended to stick to my promise.

"Now, you get on with yourself," Azalea said, and for a moment I thought she meant me. She had spoken to Ramses, however, and made a shooing motion with her hands.

"I'll take him upstairs with me while I freshen up for dinner." I scooped Ramses up and held him to my chest. He rewarded me by licking my chin. Diesel warbled at us, not happy at this attention to Ramses. "Who's in for dinner tonight?"

"Everybody," Azalea said. "Be ready in a few minutes. You might holler up at those boys and tell them to come on down."

"I will. Come on, Diesel," I said.

I climbed halfway up the stairs to the third floor and called out to Stewart and Haskell. The latter poked his head out of the door of their suite and said, "Hey, Charlie. What's up?"

"Azalea asked me to tell you *boys* that dinner will be ready in a few minutes," I said with a grin.

Haskell laughed. "Right. I'll let the other boy know." His head disappeared, and I went back down to the second floor and my own bedroom.

I put Ramses on the bed and shut the door. He immediately rolled over onto his back and enticed me to rub his belly. "You're a sponge," I told him as I complied. "A silly sponge, soaking up attention." He purred in response.

He would have let me rub his belly for several minutes, but I didn't want to keep Azalea waiting. "That's enough." I went to wash my hands and change my shoes for more comfortable slippers. We headed back down to the kitchen. I heard Stewart and Haskell on the stairs behind us. Dante barked and bounded down to play with Ramses and Diesel.

I beheld a feast on the table when I entered the kitchen. A platter of fried chicken, rice, homemade biscuits, cream gravy, green beans, and creamed corn. I felt the pounds attaching themselves to me simply by looking at the food. If I had to name a favorite meal that Azalea cooked, this would be it.

Stewart and Haskell stepped past me into the kitchen. Stewart whistled in happy surprise. "You didn't tell me we were having your amazing fried chicken tonight, Azalea. I feel like I've died and gone to heaven."

Azalea wagged a finger at him. "I know you like my fried chicken, but don't be talking about dying like that. I don't like it one little bit."

"Yes, ma'am." Stewart sounded contrite.

"Yes, you heathen. Listen to the lady." Haskell punched his partner lightly on the arm. He pulled out a chair and seated himself at his usual place.

Stewart and I took our places, but we had to calm our respective pets, thanks to the aroma of the chicken. Dante sat by Stewart and barked, and Diesel placed a large paw on my thigh. Ramses tried to jump on the table, but I discouraged him as gently as I could.

"Thank you, Azalea," I said. "Looks wonderful, as always."

"Y'all go ahead and get started," Azalea said. "I've got to be on my way. There're brownies on the counter, and ice cream in the freezer, if you feel up to having some dessert."

Haskell groaned. "Now I have to decide between your brownies and your biscuits. I

91

shouldn't have both." Then he grinned. "But I think I will."

We bade Azalea goodbye as we loaded our plates. Ramses started to follow her to the door because he sometimes went home with her. Evidently the aroma of fried chicken exerted more influence at the moment, because he turned and came back to the table to sit on the floor beside me.

I eyed Stewart and Haskell with envy as they loaded their plates. They worked out frequently at the gym and burned off a lot of calories. Unlike me. I groaned.

Stewart wagged a finger at me, in imitation of Azalea. "Now, don't you be groaning, mister. You could get yourself into the gym with Haskell and me and work off a few pounds anytime you want to."

"I know," I said as I spooned thick, delicious gravy over my biscuits and rice. Then, not so gently reminded by the felines on either side of me, I tore bits off my chicken breast and gave Diesel and Ramses a couple of bites.

Stewart let the subject drop, for which I was grateful. I felt guilty enough as it was. We ate in silence for several minutes before Stewart spoke again.

"Did you go to rehearsal this afternoon?"

I nodded. "Yes, they were blocking today."

I didn't have to translate for Stewart, who was a huge theater fan, nor for Haskell, who often accompanied Stewart to plays.

"Did the great Edmund Kean behave himself?" Stewart arched an eyebrow.

"Who is Edmund Kean?" Haskell frowned. "I thought the guy's name was Lombardi."

I wanted enlightenment as well. I knew I'd heard the name, but I couldn't recall who Edmund Kean was.

"English actor," Stewart said. "Eminent Shakespearian. Born in the late eighteenth century. Died at age forty-five, I think."

He paused for a mouthful of creamed corn. Once he finished it, he continued. "He was a short man and led a tumultuous life. I think there was a scandalous divorce as well, but I don't recall any of the circumstances."

"Lombardi isn't particularly short," I said, "but I think he leads a pretty tumultuous life. Don't know about any scandalous divorces, unless you count Madame du Jardin and her ex-husband, Anton." I then explained who they were.

"Sounds like an interesting trio," Stewart said.

"Exhausting is more like it," I replied.

My cell phone buzzed in my pocket, and I

pulled it out. Laura was calling.

"Hi, sweetheart," I said. "Is rehearsal over? I hope you don't mind that I left early."

"Just as well you did," Laura said, her tone grim. "We're having major histrionics here."

"What happened?"

Laura sighed heavily. "Oh, someone left a dead snake in Luke's dressing room, that's all, and he nearly had a heart attack when he saw it."

NINE

I sympathized with Luke Lombardi. I've loathed snakes all my life. I couldn't stand the sight of them, even on television. If I found one in the house, there was no telling how I'd react.

"You know how I feel about snakes," I said. "I feel sorry for the guy. How is he?"

"I can't stand snakes, either. We finally seem to have him calmed down," Laura said. "He's been threatening to sue everyone in sight, though."

"Any idea who the prankster is?" I asked.

"Not so far," Laura said. "The students all seem as shocked as Frank and me, so I don't think any of them is responsible."

"What about Madame du Jardin and Anton?" I suddenly remembered that I hadn't seen either of them at the theater.

"We never saw them," Laura said. "According to Luke, they don't accompany him to the theater for this stage of rehearsals."

She paused. "Do you really think one of them could have done this? Where on earth would they find a snake?"

"The weather has been warm enough lately that they're probably out. We've had a lot of sun recently," I said. "I suppose someone could have found one in a wooded area or in the park." I thought for a moment. "Then there's also the pet store. They sell snakes as pets, I believe."

"It wasn't a very big snake," Laura said. "I think you might be right about the pet store." She sighed heavily. "Now I have to get back to Luke and try to convince him he's not going to die."

I wished her luck, and we ended the call. I put my phone down on the table, and Stewart said, "What's this about snakes?"

I explained, and Stewart grimaced. Haskell frowned. "That's a nasty thing to do to someone. Whoever it was must have known this guy is afraid of snakes. How would anyone know that?"

"Maybe it's mentioned in articles about him," Stewart said. "A journalist might have asked him about his phobias, his likes and dislikes. The kind of innocuous thing they ask to fill out an interview."

"I guess," Haskell said, but he didn't appear convinced.

"Stewart's probably right," I said, "but you still have to wonder about the motive for doing this. Someone obviously has a grudge against the man, but who? The only people in town who know him are Laura, the man's mistress, and his dresser." I told them about the scenes Helen Louise and I had witnessed Saturday night.

"So Madame could have persuaded Anton to go out and find a snake, kill it, and leave it for Lombardi to find." Stewart looked thoughtful. "I can see that. The jealous Frenchwoman getting back at a faithless lover."

"Sounds like a bad movie," Haskell said.

"Some people *live* in a bad movie," Stewart retorted, "especially characters like Lombardi and his so-called entourage."

"Can't argue with that," Haskell conceded.

"I hope they can get Lombardi calmed down enough so they can get on with rehearsal," I said. "Frank and Laura don't need any added stress." I couldn't tell them about Miss An'gel's stratagem to keep Lombardi in line, but I knew they would both find it amusing. Once the play was over, I would share it with them.

"No, I imagine there's stress enough in putting on a play," Haskell said.

"Emotions are heightened, and all the cast members are worried about remembering their lines, making the right movements, and so on," Stewart said, "especially the students."

I remembered then that Stewart had participated as an undergraduate at Athena in two plays, though that was after my time there. He had mentioned his experiences on a couple of occasions. He had been interested in acting in his youth, but chemistry proved a much stronger lure as a lifelong interest.

"Haskell, from your professional point of view," I said, as a feeling of unease struck me, "is this simply a prank, or could there be a more sinister motive behind it?"

"Like what?" Stewart asked as he slipped Dante a morsel of fried chicken.

"Like someone trying to sabotage the play and keep it from taking place?" Haskell asked.

I nodded. "That's one of the possibilities that occurred to me."

"What's the other?" Haskell asked.

"Do you think someone is gunning for Luke Lombardi?" Stewart asked at the same time.

"What Stewart said," I replied. "This could be the first incident in a campaign against Lombardi, with the play simply a casualty." A thought struck me. "Make this the second incident." I told them about the pig ears being served to Lombardi at the reception. They both laughed.

"So who was going to make a silk purse out of the pig's ears?" Stewart snorted. "I think your imagination is getting the better of you," Stewart said. "What do you think?" He addressed his partner.

Haskell shrugged. "I think it's most likely some kid with an underdeveloped sense of humor. A kid who wouldn't necessarily have to know about the guy's fear of snakes. Most people wouldn't be happy to find one. Would you?"

Stewart's expression twisted into a grimace of distaste. "No, I wouldn't."

"The only thing they can do is stay alert for any further pranks," Haskell went on. "If this person is intent on screwing up the play, something else will happen soon, and not necessarily to Lombardi."

"That's not a comforting thought," I said, "but I understand the logic of it. I will discuss this with Laura and Frank, although they've probably already thought of it for themselves."

"I've got some time off due me," Haskell said, a chicken leg halfway to his mouth. He set it down. "I could show up in uniform tomorrow afternoon, make sure everyone sees me, and hang around for a while. Maybe it would put the joker off."

"That's kind of you," I said. "If you really wouldn't mind, I think it's a great idea. I can't see that Frank would object, and Lombardi might see it as a bonus for his sake."

Haskell nodded. "Right. Then I'll call Kanesha after dinner and square it with her."

Stewart beamed at me. "Isn't he the best?"

I smiled. "Yes, he is."

Haskell made a good show of ignoring us. I knew he felt uncomfortable with praise. He was a great guy, but he tended to hide behind the stone-faced expression he had perfected during his years as a sheriff's deputy. Stewart and I exchanged a knowing glance and tacitly agreed to change the subject.

We chatted in desultory fashion the rest of the meal. When we reached the dessert stage, I decided reluctantly to forgo the brownies and ice cream. Stewart and Haskell served themselves. Dante sat and whimpered next to Stewart's chair.

"I'll let you lick the bowl," he said to the dog. "You know you can't have chocolate."

Dante whined.

Ramses, seeing that I was not eating, transferred his attention to Haskell, who had been known to slip him a bite or two of food. Haskell ignored him. Diesel did not deign to beg from either of the other men. Instead he ambled into the utility room and stayed there for several minutes.

When he finished his dessert, Haskell pulled out his phone and called Kanesha. When she answered, he briefly described the situation, and she agreed to his request to take a couple of days off. Evidently things were fairly quiet in the county at the moment, but I knew that could change in an instant.

Haskell put his phone away. "All set," he said.

"That's great. Thank you so much," I replied. "I'll call Laura and let her know. I'm sure they'll appreciate it."

Haskell nodded as he got up from the table and began to clear the plates away. I helped him while Stewart finished his dessert. There was very little food left to be put away, but once that was done, Haskell and Stewart bade me good night and headed back upstairs to their suite, along with a happy Dante, who had licked up a nice bit of ice cream before Stewart put his bowl in the dishwasher.

I picked up my phone to call Laura. The call went to voice mail. She was probably onstage and couldn't answer. I would try again in a while. In the meantime I decided to call Sean and check in to see how he, Alex, and baby Rosie were doing. I had seen them all yesterday at our weekly family meal, but I liked to talk to my children every day, if possible.

"Hi, Dad. What's up?" Sean said.

"Not much. Just wanted to check in and see how y'all are doing," I replied.

"All good here. Alex is giving Rosie her dinner, and I'm sitting out on the back porch, enjoying a cigar," he said.

"Alex and the baby aren't with you, are they?" I wished he wouldn't smoke, but I knew he didn't do it that often these days. He claimed it relaxed him, and given how hard he worked, I felt I couldn't carp at him.

"No, of course not," Sean said, his tone only mildly impatient.

"Did you have a rough day at the office?" He and Alex were partners in what had been Alex's father's law firm. Alex was still on maternity leave, however, and Sean had even more to do.

"Not too bad," Sean said. "In fact, things are about to get easier. We've hired another lawyer to join the firm."

"That's great." I knew they had been considering that, but I hadn't heard any more about it for several weeks. "Who is it?"

"Her name is Anne Kimbol," Sean said. "Another transplant from Texas. I knew her briefly when I was in Houston."

"When does she start?"

"In a couple of weeks. She's got to move herself and her dogs here."

"So she's an animal person," I said. That pleased me. "What kind of dogs does she have?"

"Pugs, I believe, both rescues," Sean replied. "She's quite the animal advocate. Her specialties are family and health-care law, so Alex and I think she'll fit right in here. She was tired of big-city life in Houston, and she has a few cousins scattered here and there in Mississippi."

"I look forward to meeting her." I remembered the question I had wanted to ask him. "Does the name Finnegan Zwake mean anything to you?"

"Finnegan Zwake," Sean repeated slowly. He was silent for several seconds. "It rings a bell. Let me see. Yeah, now I've got it. That was the name of a character in a series of mysteries I read as a kid. He lived with his uncle, who was a mystery writer, and they solved murder mysteries in exotic places. Michael Dahl was the author."

"That's it." I remembered now. I had even read a couple of the books myself. "They were very good."

"They were," Sean said. "I think there were only five. So why the interest in the name?"

"That's the name of the author of the play that Frank and Laura are doing," I said. "It has to be a pseudonym, and I'll bet this guy read those same books."

"It's a mystery play, isn't it?" Sean asked.

"It is, and from what Frank and Laura have said, it's really good."

"We're looking forward to it," Sean said. "We haven't had a night out in a couple of weeks."

"I know Laura and Frank will appreciate having you attend," I said.

We chatted for a few more minutes, mostly about Rosie and Alex, and after that, I decided to move to the den to watch a little television. Diesel and Ramses accompanied me. The former immediately stretched out on the sofa, and Ramses curled up beside him. Diesel must have been in an accommodating mood, because he didn't push the kitten away, as he sometimes did.

I made myself comfortable in the recliner I had recently purchased and installed here in the den, solely for the purpose of relaxing, watching television, reading, or napping. I had done more napping than anything else, since I had a tendency to nod off while reading or watching television.

I found an old sitcom from the sixties and idly watched it. On impulse, I pulled out my phone and looked up the name Finnegan Zwake on the Internet browser. I scanned several pages of results, not one of which made any reference to the young playwright. Every link led to information about the book series and its character, as well as information about the author.

I put my phone away and stared at the television screen. As I mulled over the implications of my search, I wondered whether there was any significance to the fact that the playwright, at least under this name, had no Internet presence. Did this mean that he had only recently adopted the pseudonym?

I thought that was likely. Why was he using a fake name?

The more important question was, what was his real name?

TEN

I didn't work on Tuesdays, so I spent that morning visiting with my grandchildren at Laura and Frank's house. My children shared a nanny, a young woman named Cherelle, a relative of Azalea's who was taking online classes while earning money for continuing her education. She took turns staying at either house, and she had been a godsend when Alex was struggling with postpartum depression a few months ago. Alex had rounded the corner and was doing well, although she still had moments when the old blues threatened to descend.

Cherelle was working on her classes, and Alex had errands to run while I took care of the children. Young Charlie, Laura and Frank's son, was almost ten months old now, and his cousin, Rosie, was nearly seven months. Naturally I considered them the two most remarkable grandchildren ever born, and Charlie in particular had exhibited signs of singular precocity. He had already learned several words, including the usual *Mama* and *Dada,* along with *cat* and *Papa.* The latter referred to me, of course. He had also begun to pull himself up on things, trying to stand and walk.

Rosie's name was entirely appropriate, with her chubby little rosy cheeks and happy smile. Every time I looked at her, my heart melted. I wished her grandmother Jackie could have met her and Charlie. Aunt Dottie, too. They both loved children so much. Somehow I knew, though, that both my late wife and my aunt were never far away whenever I was with these precious mites. Charlie and Rosie had their own special guardian angels. To others that might sound like sentimental codswallop, but I took great comfort in these notions.

I stayed with the grandchildren for nearly three hours, by which time all three of us had begun to droop, me in particular. I had forgotten how much work infants could be. Alex had returned in time to give Rosie her next feeding, and I gratefully turned Charlie over to Cherelle for his latest diaper change.

Cherelle and Alex both thanked me for helping out. "You know I love doing it," I said. "No need to thank me."

Alex smiled and kissed my cheek when I bent to give her a hug. She looked so much like her old self now, for which I was deeply grateful.

"Call me if y'all need anything." I waved goodbye and headed out the front door to my car. I hadn't brought Diesel with me this morning, despite his grumbling and meowing in protest. He had remained at home with Azalea and Ramses until I was finished with my other errands.

Stops included the pharmacy, the hardware store, and the barbershop. When I left the barbershop, I sat in the car for a few minutes. I had decided to call Melba to check on her, and I didn't like talking on the phone while driving.

If I hadn't known I had dialed the correct number, I wouldn't have recognized Melba's voice when she answered. She sounded like an elderly man whose voice had roughened after years of whiskey and cigarettes.

"You don't sound good," I said.

"Course not." Melba paused to blow her nose. "I hab a code."

"Yes, sorry," I said. "Is there anything I can do for you? Bring you food, for instance?"

"Thank you," she replied. "I'd lub a quiche from the bistro."

"I'll go get one and bring it to you right now," I said. "Anything else?"

"No, dat's all." She sniffled before she ended the call.

I had forgotten to tell her that Diesel wasn't with me. I hoped she wouldn't be too disappointed not to see him. He was always good tonic when a person was ill.

At the bistro I found Melba's favorite quiche — spinach, bacon, and Gruyère cheese. The lunch crowd had begun pouring in, and Helen Louise didn't have time to talk. I managed to let her know that the babies were fine and that I was taking Melba the quiche.

"Don't catch her cold," Helen Louise said.

"I certainly won't," I said. "I'll be careful."

I paid for the quiche and went back out to my car. The drive to Melba's house took only ten minutes. I parked on the street and walked up to her door.

Melba must have been standing by the door looking out because I didn't have a chance to knock or ring the doorbell. The door opened, Melba moved back, and I stepped inside.

"Don't get any closer," Melba said. "Just set it down on the table there. Don't want you to catch my cold."

"Thanks." I placed the quiche where she had indicated. When she inquired how much she owed me, I told her not to be silly. Usually she would have argued with me and insisted on paying, but today she didn't. She must really have been sick.

"I'm sorry you're so sick," I said. "Are you sure it isn't the flu?"

"I'm sure." She pulled her flannel housecoat closer around her and shuffled into the living room in her fur-lined slippers.

I followed her, but I stopped short in the doorway. I hadn't realized she already had company. I didn't know the woman who sat on Melba's couch but she looked familiar. Melba dropped into her recliner and focused her dull gaze on me.

"Charlie, this is Katrinka Krause," Melba said. "Remember I told you about her?"

"Yes, I do." I advanced toward Ms. Krause, hand extended. By the time I reached her and she clasped my hand and smiled, I realized when and where I had seen her. She was the striking, auburn-haired woman at the reception on Saturday evening who had excited Lombardi's interest. She was the reason Madame du Jardin had created such a scene. "It's a pleasure to meet you, Ms. Krause."

"Please, call me Katrinka," she said after

she released my hand. "I feel like I know you already. Melba's always talking about her pal Charlie."

Melba blew her nose.

"We've known each other ever since elementary school," I said.

Katrinka patted the couch and indicated that I should join her.

"I would love to join you and chat awhile," I said, "but I've got to get home. Another time, perhaps."

"Certainly," Katrinka said. Melba honked into her tissues again.

Katrinka started to rise. "I can see myself out," I said. "You keep an eye on Melba here and make sure she gets over this. Without her to harass me on a daily basis, I don't know what I'd do."

Melba grimaced at me. "Ha ha."

"Bye, honey. Get well soon." I waved to her and headed for the front door.

Back in the car I drove down the street and turned toward home. I did need to get back, but I could have stayed a few minutes. The problem was Katrinka.

I remembered the story Melba had told me about her visit to New York with her friend. I also remembered what happened when they went backstage, and Luke Lombardi made advances to Katrinka. The way

Melba had told it, the advances were not welcome. Katrinka's nephew had had to intervene and ended up getting fired from the play.

At the reception, however, Katrinka seemed to welcome Lombardi's attention. What had changed in the intervening years? Why was Katrinka now interested in the actor?

The most likely explanation, I decided, was that she was attempting to help her nephew in some way. Whether she thought Lombardi had any influence with producers in New York, I didn't know. I suspected he didn't, frankly, so if that was Katrinka's goal, she would probably be disappointed.

Her other motivation could be revenge. Had she been the one who put a dead snake in his dressing room? I supposed she could easily have slipped in through one of the back entrances to the performing arts building and gained access to his dressing room without being noticed. Much of the time everyone else would have been on the stage or in the wings watching the stage.

I decided I would discuss the idea with Haskell this afternoon when Diesel and I attended the next rehearsal. He might even know Katrinka himself. He had lived and worked in Athena all his life and had as wide an acquaintance as Melba, if not wider, due to the nature of his work. Melba was in no condition to be questioned for the next few days.

I continued to think about Katrinka the rest of the drive, and by the time I reached home, I had begun to regret not staying a few more minutes at Melba's to talk to her friend. I might have been able to get her to talk to me about that trip to New York and what had happened backstage after the play. She might have let something slip about her feelings toward Luke Lombardi.

Too late now. That would have to wait. I pulled the car into the garage, retrieved my bags from the backseat, and entered the kitchen. As I could have predicted, Diesel met me and gave me a short lecture, consisting of indignant meows and insistent trills, informing me of the heinousness of his abandonment while I was larking about without him. Ramses, sitting nearby, decided to throw in a few comments of his own, while Azalea smiled at me.

"I reckon Mr. Cat is putting you in your place," she said. "Never heard a cat talk so much in my life."

"Too much, sometimes," I said. "Yes, Diesel, I'm sorry, but you couldn't come with me this morning. You'll be coming with me to the theater this afternoon, okay?"

Ramses let out an indignant squeak.

"You have to stay here," I informed him. "You're not well-behaved like Diesel. You'd get loose in that place, and we'd never find you again."

Ramses turned and walked to Azalea. He rubbed against her legs and stared at me. I had to laugh. "I think Diesel has been coaching you."

I put away the contents of my parcels, without feline assistance, and by the time I returned to the kitchen, Azalea had my lunch on the table. I enjoyed several slices of roast beef, glazed carrots, and green beans, along with a couple of pieces of cornbread. I made up for my defection this morning by sharing several tidbits of beef and a few carrot slices. That seemed to satisfy the two complainants.

Once lunch was done, I had time to relax for a bit before Diesel and I needed to head to the theater for the afternoon's rehearsal. Both my four-legged boys followed me to the den. I was surprised that Ramses didn't want to hang around Azalea, but he was smart enough to realize no more food was in the offing. He climbed onto my lap when I took my usual spot on the sofa. He turned on his back, an invitation to rub his belly.

Naturally I complied. Diesel stretched out beside us on the sofa, his head against my thigh, and I stroked him with my free hand.

While I petted the cats, I thought about Luke Lombardi and the nasty joke played on him. For no concrete reason, I was inclined to think that Katrinka Krause had something to do with the affair of the dead snake. The complete change in her attitude toward the actor between her first meeting and the latest baffled me. Why had she decided to make nice with Lombardi now?

I wanted to talk to her about this, but why should she answer my questions? She could easily tell me to mind my own business, and really, it *wasn't* my business, other than that it affected my daughter and son-in-law. Frank and Laura were capable of handling things on their own, but my paternal instincts often outweighed my judgment when it came to butting in. That was what Sean would label it.

If Melba weren't so sick with a cold, I would ask her to talk to her friend about it. While I was at Melba's, I probably should have mentioned that I'd seen Katrinka at the reception, but that could have proved awkward.

What had happened to her nephew? He was part of the original scenario. Did this

115

have anything to do with him? I realized I could ask Katrinka about her nephew, find out whether he had been able to continue his acting career after being fired from that play. What was the young man's name? Micah, that was it. I could certainly inquire about Micah, and that might lead to further information.

Pleased that I had found a conversational gambit with Katrinka, I decided I would relax and perhaps doze for a bit. I leaned back and put a cushion behind my head. Ramses and Diesel seemed content now, so I closed my eyes and drifted.

ELEVEN

I awoke to a musical sound. For a moment I couldn't remember where I was; then it came back to me. I was in the den, and I had fallen asleep. The music I heard came from my phone. I scrambled to answer it before it went to voice mail.

Laura's voice greeted me. "Dad? Where are you? Rehearsal's about to start." She sounded a bit peeved with me.

"I'm sorry, sweetheart. I dozed off in the den after lunch." I felt guilty about not setting an alarm to wake me in time. "I'll be there in a few minutes."

Laura giggled. "You're turning into a geezer, Dad. A little food, and you get sleepy."

"I'm not quite ready to be a geezer, young lady," I retorted. "Have some respect for your elders."

"That's the point, you're letting yourself get more elder all the time." I heard the

117

amusement in her voice. "Get up, and get moving."

"All right, I'm on the way." I ended the call and shifted a yawning Ramses from my lap to set him on the floor. "Come on, Diesel, time for us to go see Laura and Frank."

The Maine Coon sat up, yawned, then slid to the floor. He trotted out the door, and Ramses and I followed him to the kitchen. I noted by the kitchen clock that the time was a few minutes to three. I'd better get a move on.

Azalea emerged from the utility room with a basket of folded and dried linens. "Good nap?"

"Yes, and now I'm late," I said. "Laura just called and woke me up. Diesel and I are going to rehearsal."

"I'll look after Ramses," Azalea said.

"Thank you. Okay, Diesel, to the car. We'll see you later."

During the drive to the performing arts center on campus, Diesel must have picked up on my slight feelings of anxiety, because he warbled several times.

"Everything is okay, boy," I said. "I don't like being late when I'm supposed to be somewhere at a certain time."

He meowed as if he understood, and the warbling ceased. I grinned. Anyone who overheard these conversations I had with my cats would have thought I was more than a bit potty. At least, people who didn't have pets would have thought that. Pet owners understood.

I parked in the lot beside the performing arts center, and as I let Diesel out of the car, I glanced toward the back of the building. Struck by an idea, I headed that way instead of to the front entrance. Diesel trod alongside me, and I talked to him as we walked.

"Figured I might as well check out the entrances to the building from the back," I said. "We'll see how easy it is to get into the building without anyone seeing us. Of course, after what happened, they may have tightened things up by locking doors. But we might as well test it."

Diesel chirped in response as he usually did, and I enjoyed the illusion — or was it? — that he understood. As we rounded the corner of the structure to reach the rear of it, I headed for a point where I could examine the whole back. I could see three points of entry. One was the loading dock, and the other two were doors into different parts of the building.

I tested the loading dock first, and the doors there were locked. I figured they probably remained that way unless a delivery arrived. The first of the other doors also was locked, so I moved to the third one. This door opened readily, and Diesel and I stepped into a rehearsal room about twice the size of my spacious kitchen. Chairs and music stands stood in haphazard fashion around the room. I spied a couple of timpani in one corner along with other percussion equipment.

Double doors in one wall sat ajar, and the cat and I walked through them into a dimly lit hall. I spotted a figure walking toward us, and I recognized Haskell in uniform. I called out a greeting.

Haskell responded with "Good afternoon, guys. What are you doing back here?" He frowned. "I didn't see you come in."

Diesel and I halted near him, and I gave a sheepish grin. "Thought I'd see how easy it was to get into this building from the back without anyone seeing me. Or, rather, seeing us."

"Today it would have been harder than yesterday," he said. "Yesterday both doors were evidently unlocked, and anyone could have come in. The loading dock doors stay locked according to the building supervisor." He frowned again. "Earlier I checked back here, and both the other doors were locked then."

"That's not good," I said, feeling a little alarmed. "Any idea who came back here and unlocked the door?"

Haskell shook his head. "No. You don't need a key to unlock it from inside, but someone with a key could have come in and forgotten to lock it back. I'll ask around. I'll go secure it now." He walked past us, and we waited until he returned.

Together we headed for the front of the building toward the stage. "How are things going onstage?" I asked.

"They're going over their lines," Haskell said. "Lombardi hasn't shown up yet, and Frank isn't happy about that. Laura was going to call the hotel and find out where he is."

When we reached the auditorium, however, I heard Lombardi's booming voice in the midst of an explanation for his tardiness.

". . . drive myself, but I got a little lost, else I'd have been here on time, dear boy. Soon as I figured out where I went wrong, I turned around, and here I am."

"The main thing is you made it," Frank said. "Let's start over with the first act. Luke, you and Laura are up."

Haskell left me to continue his perambulations around the theater, and Diesel and I took the same seats we'd had the day before. I looked around for Finn Zwake, but I didn't see him in the auditorium. Perhaps he lurked backstage.

I focused on the two actors onstage. I didn't have the script to check them against, but it sounded to me as if they both knew their lines. Neither appeared to stumble as they worked their way through the scene, and I was relieved. Things seemed to be going well. I hoped nothing would happen to disturb the progress of the rehearsal today.

As I watched the two principals move around the stage as the dialogue progressed, I spotted the playwright in the wings. He stood almost onstage; otherwise I wouldn't have noticed him. He appeared absorbed in the action, and he edged a little farther onstage.

Fascinated, I continued to watch Zwake rather than Laura and Lombardi. If he kept inching forward, he would end up right in the middle of the action. Suddenly, however, his head jerked as he appeared to catch sight of something or someone, and he scuttled quickly back out of sight. I glanced around to see what or who might have startled him, and I saw Haskell in the wings on the opposite side of the stage. I checked the other side, and Zwake was no longer in sight.

Haskell appeared not to have noticed Zwake or his odd behavior, and I wondered whether it was Haskell's entrance that accounted for the playwright's disappearing. Haskell looked stern at the moment as he focused on the two actors, but what about him could have frightened Zwake? The uniform? Or did he recognize Haskell himself?

I continued to puzzle over the playwright's strange actions, particularly since he never reappeared during that day's rehearsal. If he remained in the theater, he took care to stay out of sight. His reaction to Haskell made me wonder whether Zwake had been the one to put the snake in Lombardi's dressing room. Haskell didn't know who had played the prank any more than I did.

When I talked to Haskell during a break in the stage action, I asked him whether he had noticed Zwake.

"I saw him," Haskell said. "I looked away for a moment, and when I glanced back over there again, he was gone."

"He reacted oddly when he saw you," I said. "At least, I'm pretty sure it was you that caused it." I explained what I had seen, and Haskell frowned.

"He didn't look familiar to me," Haskell

123

said. "I didn't get a close look at him, though. I might have caught him speeding once out in the county." He shrugged. "People act funny sometimes after they've been ticketed, and you run into them somewhere."

I hadn't thought of that. Maybe that was all it was. I felt almost disappointed because I'd thought the behavior had a more sinister origin.

Not every little thing is a mystery, Charlie, I reminded myself.

Diesel meowed to alert me to his presence, and I rubbed his head. He meowed again.

"Sounds like he wants something," Haskell said.

Diesel chirped loudly.

"I think you're right, and I'm pretty sure I know what it is." I checked my watch, and it was nearly five o'clock. "He wants his dinner, and frankly, I'm wanting mine."

Haskell grinned. "Y'all go on home. I'm here to keep an eye on things. No need for you to hang around."

"I'm not going to argue with you," I said. "Thanks for doing this. I appreciate it, and I know Frank and Laura do, too."

Haskell nodded. "See you later." He walked away from us, and I reckoned he was going to make his round through the backstage areas.

"Come on, boy, we're going home." Diesel led the way as we headed up the aisle toward the entrance to the theater, and we emerged into the afternoon sunlight. After my eyes adjusted, we walked around the building to the car.

On the drive home, during dinner, and throughout the following day, I occasionally thought about Finn Zwake. I saw him briefly at rehearsal the next afternoon, but when he saw me approaching him, he waved and hurried away. I took the hint. He didn't want to talk to me, and I had to wonder why. I figured he had heard about my reputation as an amateur investigator. Perhaps that was why he wanted to avoid me, but to my mind, that meant he was guilty of something. But of what?

Thursday's rehearsal was the run-through, when they did the play as a performance. I was looking forward to seeing this, since I'd not had the chance to see this aspect of putting on a play before. I didn't know how long it would take, but I was determined to stay through the whole thing. For that reason I left Diesel home with Azalea. Stewart would be there when Azalea left, and Diesel wouldn't have to miss his dinner.

The action started on a high note. I thought Lombardi and Laura played their parts tremendously well, and I glowed with pride for my daughter. They finished the first scene and moved on to the next one.

About forty-five minutes later, the first act concluded, and Frank had a few directions for members of the cast, chiefly the students. One of them had flubbed a cue, and Frank spoke with firm patience to the young woman about it. Lombardi had disappeared from the stage while this was going on, but Laura remained present.

While stagehands readied the set for the beginning of the second act, I checked my phone for messages and e-mails. I had turned the sound off after I arrived in the theater. I found a text message from Melba from over an hour ago.

Feeling much better. Will be back in the office tomorrow.

I texted back, urging her to take the day off and rest.

She responded quickly.

Bored to death here. See you tomorrow.

I texted back. *Okay, see you then.*

I scanned my e-mails, but none required an immediate response. I put my phone away and focused on the stage again.

The stage crew had finished, and Frank

126

was rounding up the players for the beginning of the second act. Everyone except Luke Lombardi was present, but he turned up after only about three minutes' wait. Frank frowned at him but forbore to speak to Lombardi about his tardiness.

"Places, everyone," Frank called out.

Laura and Lombardi moved to their spots onstage, along with the young woman playing their maid. I thought her name was Agnes, but that might have been the name of her character. I couldn't remember.

"Okay, the curtain is coming up." Frank moved off the stage and walked to his spot in the first row of seats. "Action."

Agnes walked onstage and headed for Laura, who stood by a drinks cabinet. Agnes bore a tray with a bottle of what might have been whiskey but was more likely tea, along with a couple of glasses. She set it down on top of the cabinet.

"Thank you, Agnes," Laura said. "That will be all for now."

"Yes, ma'am," Agnes replied, then turned away and exited the stage.

"Your usual, darling?" Laura asked, with a fulsome glance at Lombardi. At this point in the play, Laura's character was increasingly on edge over what she suspected was the plot to kill her.

Lombardi made a careless gesture. "What else? Surely after all this time you know exactly what I want." His tone grew sharper with each word.

Laura matched his tone. "I'm afraid I do." She turned her back to the audience as she poured the liquid into the glasses. When she finished, she picked up one and carried it to Lombardi. Their faces in profile to the audience, they eyed each other hostilely for a long moment; then Lombardi lifted the glass as if in a toast.

Laura watched intently. Lombardi tossed back the liquid in the manner of a practiced tippler. Lombardi swallowed.

Then he started coughing, his face turning rapidly red. He gasped for air.

I was startled. I didn't remember this from the perusal of the script I had done last night.

"Luke, what's the matter?" Laura sounded frantic. "Frank, come here. Now. He can't breathe."

Twelve

I sat and watched Luke Lombardi dying right before my eyes.

Haskell and Frank reached the actor at nearly the same time. Haskell had his phone to his ear and barked into it. I could hear him clearly. He ordered an ambulance and backup.

Laura tried to unbutton Lombardi's shirt, but his flailing arms obstructed her. As this continued, I began to realize that he perhaps wasn't dying after all.

Frank bellowed for water as he supported the weakened man to a chair. Moments later a stagehand rushed in with a glass, and Lombardi grabbed it and gulped down the contents. Everyone watched as slowly the man's natural color returned. All except Laura. I saw her sniffing at her own glass and then take a tentative sip. She grimaced and set the glass down.

"What happened?" Frank asked Lombardi.

"Hot," Lombardi said, his voice hoarse and ragged. "Burned going down."

"There's something incredibly hot in the tea," Laura said. "I suspect something like a Carolina Reaper or a habanero." She grimaced again. "My tongue is burning from just a tiny sip."

"Water isn't the way to recover from a hot pepper," Haskell said. "He needs milk or something greasy to eat."

One of the cast members, a lanky young man of about twenty, stepped forward and held out a bag. "I've got a bottle of milk. He's welcome to it."

"Thanks, Todd," Frank said as he accepted the bag. He withdrew a plastic bottle of milk, opened it, and handed it to Lombardi. "Drink this."

Lombardi didn't argue. He downed the pint of milk in several gulps. He handed the empty container to Frank.

"Did that help?" Laura asked.

Lombardi turned on her, and the anger in his expression made Laura step back. "You couldn't help yourself, could you? You had to play another trick on me. You want me to embarrass myself in front of the Broadway director who's coming to see me."

Though his voice still had a hoarse edge, he had recovered remarkably. His accusation stunned me, and I was out of my seat and headed for the stage before I realized what I was doing.

Laura's expression turned stormy. "That is absolutely the most asinine thing I've ever heard you say, you idiot. Why should I want to embarrass you when you're more than capable of doing it yourself? They could can you and sell you as Parma ham any day of the week. Don't you dare sit there and accuse me of something so unbelievably crass and stupid. You aren't worth the effort as far as I'm concerned."

My daughter, like her father, had a hair-trigger temper sometimes. Lombardi had hit that trigger, hard. He recoiled briefly in the face of her fury, but when Laura ceased talking, he was ready for another attack.

"You should stick to having babies. That's all you're fit for. You're an embarrassment on the stage. That's why I swore I'd never work with you again. I only did this as a favor to our mutual agent. Whom I'm going to fire, by the way, after this."

By now I had reached Laura's side. Frank started to speak, but I cut in.

"Listen to me, you has-been hack. Don't you dare talk to my daughter this way.

131

You're the one who's an embarrassment. You're upset because you know Laura is better than you, and you're terrified this director is going to see that and offer her a part and not you. If I hear one more word out of you . . ."

Laura pushed me aside. "Shut up, Dad. I can fight this turkey on my own. Listen to me, Luke, and listen good. The minute Miss An'gel hears about this, you can kiss any hopes of being seen by this director good-bye. The first thing I'm going to do the minute I leave this stage is call her and tell her what a giant jackass you're making of yourself. You understand? And if you don't, you might get something stronger onstage tomorrow night." She turned and stormed off the stage.

Lombardi sat in stunned silence. Either Laura's final threats had made an impression or he had begun to regret his tantrum as reality checked back in to his addled brain.

Frank threw an annoyed glance at me, and I realized he hadn't appreciated my outburst. "Go check on Laura," he said, and turned his attention back to Lombardi.

I decided not to argue and went to find my daughter backstage. She was in her dressing room, jerking a brush through her hair. She berated herself in the mirror, but she ceased when she saw me behind her.

"Sorry about all that." She sounded tired. I put my hands on her shoulders and gave a gentle squeeze.

"You were provoked. He had no reason whatsoever to attack you like that."

"You're right. He didn't." Laura laid the brush aside and turned to look up at me. "That's Luke in full glory. He always lashes out at someone, and I was the most convenient target. For the record, I did not put anything in that bottle of tea."

"I know you didn't." I waved that impatiently aside. "The prankster responsible for the snake did that. Did Lombardi ever accuse you of that?"

"No, he knows I don't like snakes, either," Laura said. "That's why I'm puzzled he would blame me for this latest prank."

"Are Madame and Anton around today?" I asked.

"Anton is," Laura said. "Probably in Luke's dressing room. Luke doesn't like him around when he's onstage, though sometimes Anton lurks in the wings. Why do you ask?"

"He could be the prankster," I said. "How long have he and Madame been divorced?"

"I'm not sure," Laura replied. "Not too

long, though, from what I've gathered. Luke's affair with Madame has been going on for several years, though, if that's what you're after."

"Yes," I said. "Hasn't it occurred to you that the worm — in this case, Anton — may finally have turned? That he's been burning with resentment after all this time, and he's finally decided to get back at Lombardi?"

Laura thought that over for a moment. Then she said slowly, "You could be right. I'm sure Luke told Anton and Madame what Miss An'gel said about a big Broadway name coming to the performance on Saturday evening. Luke hasn't had a really good role in a while, and this could be Anton's way of paying him back, keeping him too rattled to perform well, or at all."

"Exactly." I felt satisfied that I had finally identified the prankster. "I think I'll tell Haskell all this, and he can go and question Anton."

"Yes, let Haskell do that." Laura gazed at me sternly.

"Message received," I said. "Do you feel up to going back onstage?"

"Yes, let's go," Laura replied.

The EMTs had arrived by the time we reached the stage, and one of them was examining Lombardi. Laura and I stopped in the wings to wait until the examination concluded. After a couple of minutes, the EMT seemed satisfied.

"I don't think there's any lasting damage," she said, "but if you continue to have pain, you should go to the emergency room and get it checked out further."

"Thank you." Lombardi ran a hand over his throat. "I think it will be okay. I'm feeling much better."

"Have more milk just in case," the young woman advised.

Once the EMTs had completed their paperwork and received the necessary signatures, they cleared their equipment from the stage and departed. Laura emerged from the wings, but I stayed where I was, mindful of what she had said to me.

Lombardi came to my daughter immediately, his expression contrite. He took her hands in his. "Laura, my dear, do forgive me. I was so terrified that I would lose my voice forever that I struck out blindly. You know how important the voice is to an actor. Without it we would be nothing. You *must* say you will forgive me."

Laura stared hard at him for a good ten seconds before she pulled her hands free. "I do forgive you, Luke. But if you ever behave like that again to me or anyone involved in this production, I will move heaven and earth to get you fired. Do you understand me?"

Lombardi stiffened, and at first I thought he would react angrily. Whatever his true feelings, he evidently decided not to antagonize Laura or Frank, who stood by glaring at him. "I understand. You will not need to remind me again."

He turned to Frank. "I believe I will rest briefly in my dressing room. Anton has preparations to soothe my throat, and I should do what I can to prepare myself for the dress rehearsal tomorrow."

"That's fine," Frank said. "Your understudy can take over for now. Jared, you're on."

A tall, slightly plump young man stepped forward, his expression eager. "Yes, sir, I'm ready."

Lombardi eyed the younger actor askance but said nothing. Instead he headed into the wings where I stood, followed by Haskell. As the latter neared me, I motioned for him to wait. Once Lombardi was out of sight, I shared with Haskell my thoughts on Anton as the likely suspect for the pranks.

Haskell listened, his expression giving nothing away as usual, but he nodded when I finished. "Sounds plausible," he said. "I'll talk to Anton when I can get him away from Lombardi."

With that, I had to be content. I was about to go back to my seat in the auditorium when I caught a flash of movement in the wings on the other side of the stage. *Probably one of the stagehands,* I decided and went to my seat.

On the stage Frank called his cast to order. "Act two, second scene. Everyone in place." He was not going to go through the first scene again, and I thought that was a good idea. No need to go through that again and let the actors fixate on what had happened to Lombardi. I saw that the drinks tray had disappeared from the top of the cabinet. Presumably a stagehand had removed it and emptied the bottle as well as Laura's glass.

Or maybe Haskell had confiscated it to have it analyzed. *That's what should be done,* I thought. If the juice of a pepper accounted for the taste, and that type of pepper wasn't available locally, then Anton was most likely the prankster.

Then I remembered the local upscale grocery store that catered to the foodies in the area. I rarely shopped there, but I recalled that they carried a lot of unusual items, including numerous types of peppers, not available elsewhere in Athena. Such peppers were no doubt available in Memphis as well, and in Memphis no one was going to remember someone who bought a particular pepper. Anton would have had to be absent from the hotel in Memphis for an appreciable amount of time in order to go grocery shopping, surely, and that would have been noticed.

Haskell should be the one to ask the questions, not me, I reminded myself. Frank, as the director and producer of the play, also had authority because of his roles. He, after all, was responsible for the welfare of his cast and crew during the duration of rehearsals and performances. I knew he took his duties seriously and would do his best to discover the identity of the prankster before anything worse occurred.

I sat back and focused on the run-through of the second act. Young Jared, the understudy, had his teeth in the role, and after watching him for a few minutes, I decided that, should Lombardi be unable to go on, Jared ought to do just fine in the role. He and Laura played well off each other.

With my peripheral vision, I glimpsed a person walk past me down toward the front of the auditorium. I turned my head to get a full look. The newcomer was not Finn

138

Zwake, as I'd hoped, but a young man I'd not seen before that I could recall.

He watched the action onstage intently, and a couple of times I saw him nod, as if in approval. A few minutes later, Frank called a halt to correct an issue one of the secondary players was having with her line, and the young man took the opportunity to climb onstage.

Frank frowned when he noticed the newcomer but didn't stop his work with the young woman. When she assured him she understood exactly what he wanted, he nodded and moved aside, ready to resume.

The stranger stepped forward and extended a hand to my son-in-law. "I'm sorry to interrupt. Looks like you're doing the run-through, and from what I've seen, it's going to be an excellent production. I'm Finnegan Zwake, and I guess you must be Frank Salisbury, the director and producer."

THIRTEEN

A second Finnegan Zwake? What the heck was going on here?

Up on the stage, Frank looked every bit as confused as I felt. He eyed the young stranger warily.

"Excuse me. Would you remind repeating that?" Frank said. Everyone else onstage watched and waited for the response.

The young man shifted, perhaps a bit uneasy. "I'm Finnegan Zwake, the author of the play. You know, the one you're rehearsing right now?" He glanced around the stage. "What's going on here? I don't understand."

"You're Finnegan Zwake," Frank said.

"Yeah," the stranger said. "I mean, it's not my real name, of course. I use it for my writing. It's a lot cooler than my own name."

"What is your real name?" Frank asked.

The young man appeared to hesitate, and when he spoke, he sounded defensive.

"Ulrich Zwingli Dingelbach."

A giggle escaped someone onstage but was quickly cut off.

No wonder the poor boy used a pseudonym, I thought. The name Ulrich Zwingli sounded familiar, and I tried in vain to remember why.

Frank appeared incredulous, as if he thought the young man was pranking him, and his expression darkened. "Now, listen here, what's your name? I'm too busy to be yanked around with some ridiculous story."

"This isn't a story. I've told you my real name, and I *am* Finnegan Zwake. Why don't *you* stop jerking me around and tell me what the hell is going on here?" The would-be Zwake had shifted position, and I could now see him in profile. He was every bit as angry as my son-in-law.

Frank appeared to realize the young man meant what he had said about his identity. "Look here, Dingelbach, this is what I don't understand. I've already met and talked to Finn Zwake, and the guy I talked to isn't you. He's about five inches taller, and he has fiery red hair and a big mustache."

"I don't know who this guy is, but he's yanking your chain," Dingelbach replied with some heat. He reached in his jacket pocket and pulled out a wallet. He dug out a card and presented it to Frank. It was the size and shape of a driver's license.

Frank took the card and stared hard at it. Then he handed it back to the young man. "It says you're Ulrich Z. Dingelbach. But it doesn't prove you're Finn Zwake."

With a flourish, the young man pulled an envelope from the same jacket pocket and presented it to my son-in-law. "Read this."

Frank accepted the envelope, opened it, and pulled out a folded piece of paper. Once he had unfolded it, he began to read its contents. I was so curious, I wanted to run up onstage and grab the letter from Frank's hands. What did it say?

"Do you believe me now?" Dingelbach said, a note of triumph in his voice.

Frank lowered the letter and fixed Dingelbach with his sternest gaze. "If this isn't a forgery, then you are who you say you are, Dingelbach. And you are the real Finnegan Zwake to boot."

"It's not a forgery," Dingelbach said. "As you can see, that letter is from my agent. I imagine you recognize the name."

Frank nodded.

"I'd hardly go around forging letters with her name on them," Dingelbach said. "I'd be hip deep in hyena poop before I knew it."

I frowned. I'd heard that *hip deep in hyena poop* phrase earlier. It was in the first act of the play. This young man, I decided, was the real Finnegan Zwake. That line was too distinctive and came too easily from his tongue for him not to be the genuine article.

Apparently this convinced Frank as well. Laura, who had stood by during the whole exchange, stepped forward. "Do you have any idea why someone would claim to be you?" Laura asked. "And why haven't you appeared before now? Why wait until a couple of days before the performance?"

Dingelbach shook his head. "I have no idea who the guy is, but I'm looking forward to meeting him. As to the reason why I just turned up today, I've been out of the country the past couple of weeks. I was in the Highlands of Scotland researching a new play I'm hoping to write. I got back to New York yesterday afternoon and found that letter waiting for me. So I hopped the first plane for Memphis today and drove down from there."

Dingelbach's story sounded eminently plausible. I hadn't heard much about the other Finnegan Zwake, other than that he was supposed to be from somewhere around here. Dingelbach did have traces of a Mississippi drawl, I realized, and I had a further realization. The surname Dingelbach was familiar.

When I had been a student at Athena many years ago, there was a history professor named Dingelbach. His specialty was the Reformation, and I then recalled where I had heard the name Ulrich Zwingli.

I got up from my seat and approached the stage. "Excuse me, Mr. Dingelbach. Was your father a history professor?"

Dingelbach turned to look down at me. "Yes, he was. He taught here as a matter of fact. He's the one who named me."

"He taught courses on the Reformation," I said. "I took one of them when I was a junior. As I recall, he was passionately interested in his field."

Dingelbach offered a wry grin. "So passionate, in fact, that he named me after the subject of his major work."

"That's where I heard it," Laura said, her eyes lighting with excitement. "The leader of the Reformation in Switzerland. I read your dad's biography of Zwingli for a class in college. Not here," she added. "I didn't know your father personally."

"How is your father these days?" I asked. "Is he still with us?"

Dingelbach shook his head. "No, my dad died about fifteen years ago, when I was nearly fourteen. Mom died a few years later. They had me when they were in their late forties."

"I'm sorry for your loss," I said. "I liked your father."

"Thank you," Dingelbach said. "He was a great guy, despite the name he zapped me with." He grinned suddenly, and I could see the real affection he had for his father's memory.

Frank called a halt to the discussion. "Look, we've got a run-through to finish here, and I'd like to get it done before midnight." He returned the letter to Dingelbach. "You and I can discuss this later, but right now I'd like you off the stage." He smiled to remove any sting from the words.

"Absolutely," Dingelbach said. "I had no idea introducing myself would cause such a kerfuffle." He laughed as he exited the stage to take the seat next to me.

I quickly introduced myself as the action got under way. I explained my relationship to Frank and Laura.

"Nice to meet you," Dingelbach said, his attention focused on the stage. He extracted a notebook and pen from another pocket, preparing to jot down notes, I presumed.

During the hour that followed, I never saw him make a note. I took that as a sign that he was pleased with both Frank's direction and the actors' performances. Luke Lombardi reappeared twenty minutes after the run-through resumed and took his role over from an obviously disappointed Jared.

I watched for Dingelbach's reaction to Lombardi's performance. Lombardi's voice sounded fine, I thought, almost as if he hadn't swallowed that fiery glass of pepper-infused tea. Anton's remedy had done its magic.

Dingelbach frowned at Lombardi's first few lines, but then his lips relaxed. I turned my attention back to the stage. The run-through proceeded smoothly with no further interruptions. Although I had read the play and knew what was coming, I still felt the thrill of the buildup to the climax when Laura's character murdered her husband by stabbing him repeatedly in the chest. There was no blood in this performance as there would be on the night when the audience was in place. When the action ended, Frank stepped forward to compliment the cast and crew. He also had a few more instructions to give, and beside me I saw Dingelbach nod. He put away his notebook and pen.

I saw Lombardi rubbing his chest and frowning in Laura's direction, and I suspected my daughter had been a bit too enthusiastic when she was stabbing Lombardi. The actor didn't say anything, at least not then. Laura shared with me later that he had been testy with her backstage, but she had apologized sweetly enough that he got over his irritation.

"Are you pleased with this production?" I asked Dingelbach.

"What I've seen of it, I certainly am," he replied. "Your son-in-law is an excellent director, and your daughter is great in this role. I loved the frenzy at the end when she was stabbing her husband. It was chilling."

I could have enlightened him on Laura's *frenzy* but chose not to. I would share this with her, however, and hoped she would duplicate it in the public performance. "Thank you. They're both talented. Laura spent some time in Hollywood and also in summer stock in the East before she decided to settle down here."

"I can believe it." He grinned suddenly. "I'm sorry she's married, though. She's gorgeous."

I laughed. "Yes, and she has a child, too, my grandson."

"Don't worry," Dingelbach said. "Married is not my type. If you'll excuse me, I really want to talk to Frank."

"Go right ahead." I thought about waiting

147

around to speak to Laura but decided instead to go in search of Haskell. I had been so absorbed in the run-through that I had forgotten about his plan to talk to Anton. Now I was curious to find out what he had learned.

I found him in the corridor where the dressing rooms were located, coming out of the men's room.

"I was about to come find you," Haskell said.

"How did it go with Anton?" I walked alongside him as he headed for the stage area.

"Fine," he said. "I talked to him about the pranks, and he got pretty indignant. Swore undying loyalty to Lombardi. He just shrugged when I asked him about his ex-wife and Lombardi. Basically I got the impression that he didn't care one way or another."

"Odd," I said.

"You're telling me," Haskell said. "I don't get these people at all."

"Do you think he's behind the pranks?" I asked.

"No, I don't think so," Haskell said. "Even though he had the opportunity. I asked him if he'd done any pepper shopping in Memphis or here, and he swore up and down he hadn't. I believed him."

"If you believed him, then I guess I do, too," I said. "You've got too much experience to be taken in."

Haskell shrugged. "I'm not always right, but I feel pretty sure. Unless this guy is an even better actor than his boss."

By now we had reached the wings, and we paused to see what was going on. Frank stood downstage talking to Laura, Dingelbach, and Lombardi while the rest of the cast and crew chatted in small groups of three or four.

"Who's the stranger?" Haskell asked. "I saw him sitting with you earlier."

"You missed the big entrance." I chuckled. "He had us all in a tizzy. He's the real Finnegan Zwake. The other one is an impostor. Frank will have to check this guy's story out, but he seems legitimate to me."

"What the heck is going on here?" Haskell said. "Is the theater always this nuts behind the scenes?"

"Maybe it is," I replied. "I don't know. You'll have to ask Laura and Frank about it. Anyway, *this* Finnegan Zwake shared his real name, unlike the other one. Ulrich Zwingli Dingelbach."

Haskell eyed me with suspicion. "Are you sure this isn't another prank? Who has a name like, well, whatever you said?"

I explained the origin of the young man's unusual name, and that seemed to mollify Haskell a bit. "Now that you mention it, I remember the professor." He grinned. "Had to slow him down a couple of times. He loved to drive like a bat out of hell on the back roads. I vaguely remember he had a kid in the car with him on one occasion. Poor kid looked scared to death."

"I can imagine," I said.

"So this guy is that kid," Haskell said. "That ought to be easy enough to check. He sounds legit to me."

"Me, too," I said. "The question now is, who the heck is the other guy going around claiming he's Finn Zwake?"

"The next time you see him, if I'm around, point him out, and I'll find out," Haskell said.

"Well, here's your chance." I pointed to the man I had just spotted walking down the aisle toward the stage, all unaware, I presumed, that his masquerade had derailed.

FOURTEEN

Haskell stepped forward onto the stage and into the light, and the fake Finn Zwake looked up and saw him. He did an immediate about-face and headed back the way he had come. Haskell called out to him, but Zwake sped up and quickly disappeared from sight through the doors.

I watched as Haskell exited the stage and ran after him. I waited, expecting to see him return any moment with Zwake in tow. When Haskell did return a few minutes later, he was alone.

Everyone else onstage apparently had been too absorbed in their own conversations to notice what was going on. I left the stage and met Haskell in front of it.

"No luck, I guess." I grimaced.

Haskell shook his head. "No, by the time I got out the front doors, he was nowhere in sight. I looked around, thinking he might be hiding nearby, but there was no sign of him. Not even a car driving off."

"Better luck next time," I said. "He's bound to turn up again before long. Unless he knows the real Finn by sight, he's not yet aware that he's been exposed as a fraud."

"Why would he run off the minute he sees a guy in uniform?" Haskell asked. "Why is he so afraid of a law officer?"

"I don't know, unless he has outstanding warrants somewhere," I replied. "That would be incentive to keep away from the law, I'd say."

"Yes," Haskell said. "But unless he's on some major wanted list that's circulated around the country, no law officer is going to automatically assume he's on the run. His behavior is peculiar."

"I can't argue with that," I said. "Now that the real Finn has turned up, I'm puzzled as to why fake Finn even tried this in the first place. Did he somehow know that real Finn wasn't going to be around, or was he simply gambling that the actual writer of the play would be busy somewhere else and wouldn't bother to come to see a regional performance?"

"Not a clue," Haskell said. "Good questions I'd like to ask him when we finally do track him down."

"What are you two discussing so intently?"

Haskell and I looked up to see Frank at the edge of the stage peering down at us. I explained what had happened, and Frank nodded.

"That settles it for me," he said. "If that guy was the real deal, he wouldn't hoof it the moment he saw Haskell. Dingelbach is the real Zwake."

"What's that?" Dingelbach had joined Frank at the stage edge.

"The impostor showed up a few minutes ago," I said. "But when he spotted Haskell here, he took off." I introduced the two men, and Haskell related his story of having ticketed Dingelbach's father.

The young man grinned. "Dad was a speed demon, and he terrified me every time I got in the car with him. I was glad that day you stopped him. He never drove that way with me in the car again."

"Just doing my job," Haskell replied. "Did you happen to see your impostor?"

"No, I didn't," Dingelbach said. "I think I must have been standing with my back to the house when he appeared."

"Frank, what about you?" Haskell asked.

"I didn't notice him, either. I didn't even see you go after him," Frank said. "We were too involved in our discussion."

"Where's Laura?" I stepped away to scan

153

the stage behind Frank and the playwright. "I don't see her, or Lombardi, either. They must have gone to their dressing rooms."

"I doubt they saw the man, either," Frank said, "but I'll go check with them."

"I'll come with you," Dingelbach said. "I'd like to talk to Luke Lombardi again."

"If you don't mind, Frank," I said, "I think I'll head home. It's way past my dinnertime."

Frank laughed. "Thanks for being here, Charlie. You go on home and enjoy your meal."

Dingelbach nodded goodbye, and he and Frank disappeared into the wings.

"Tell Stewart, if you don't mind, that I'll be home in an hour, probably," Haskell said. "See you later."

My stomach grumbled as I drove home through the dusky evening. I was such a creature of habit when it came to eating. I liked my meals at the same time every day, or close to it. I could survive the occasional interruption of my schedule, I reminded myself.

Stewart, Dante, Ramses, and Diesel greeted me when I walked into the kitchen a few minutes later.

"I was beginning to wonder what was going on," Stewart said. "I expected you back

154

here at least half an hour ago. Anything happen?"

I moved to the sink to wash my hands after quick rubs on the heads of all three pets. "Yes, as a matter of fact. The real Finnegan Zwake turned up at the run-through."

"The real Finnegan Zwake?" Stewart looked puzzled.

"Yes, apparently the guy who showed up at the reception and then later at the theater is an impostor. The real playwright was out of the country until yesterday and found a letter from his agent waiting for him, telling him about the production of the play. He flew to Memphis today from New York and drove down."

"And you're sure this second man is the real thing?" Stewart removed a plate from the oven and set it at my usual place at the table. He sat across from me and pulled Dante into his lap.

"Pretty sure." I took my seat and examined the plate. Baked chicken breast, mashed potatoes and gravy, English peas, and a large slice of cornbread. I dug in.

Diesel placed a large paw on my thigh, as he did at every meal I ate in this kitchen. Ramses sat on the other side and begged as well.

"Don't let them con you into giving them

any food," Stewart said with a grin. "They've already had more than enough."

"You heard what Stewart said." I gave Diesel a stern look, and after a moment he withdrew his paw. I tried the same tactic with Ramses, but to no avail.

"I should have named you Incorrigible," I said to Ramses. He responded with an enthusiastic meow, as if I had promised him food.

Stewart laughed. "That name would certainly fit him, although Ramses the Great would be even better."

"Please, he doesn't need any encouragement," I said.

"He can't have any of the chicken anyway," Stewart said. "Azalea seasoned it with garlic and onion powder."

I nodded. I picked out two buttery English peas and offered them to Ramses. He sniffed at them and licked the butter from them, and that seemed to satisfy him. I placed the two rejected peas on the edge of my plate.

"That's all you get," I told him. He sat in silence and watched me eat the rest of my meal.

"So tell me about the real Finnegan Zwake," Stewart said.

"His real name is Ulrich Zwingli Dingelbach," I said.

Stewart crowed with laughter. "I remember that poor kid. His father was a history professor at the college. I couldn't believe anyone would saddle a kid with a name like that."

"Yes, I agree with you," I said.

Stewart sobered. "He's got to be about thirty now, I'd say. I don't know what happened to him after his father died. He must have moved away. I think his mother was still alive, though."

"According to Dingelbach, his mother died a few years after his father, so I suppose he would have been about eighteen then," I said.

"Old enough to be on his own, I guess," Stewart said. "I hope there was other family somewhere, poor kid."

"That, I don't know," I replied. "I'm sure you'll get a chance to meet him, if you'd like to."

Stewart nodded. "I liked his father a lot, even though he almost failed me in Western Civ." He shook his head. "I was a freshman and thought I knew everything. Dr. Dingelbach quickly convinced me I didn't. Ah, the arrogance of youth."

"I vaguely remember," I said. "My own youth, that is."

Stewart grinned at me. "So many decades ago." Before I could respond, he continued. "What's the word with Helen Louise? I imagine she's staying busy with Henry on vacation."

"She is, and she's reveling in it," I said. "She appreciates Henry — don't get me wrong — and she relies on him. But at heart she's a workaholic."

"So you've hardly talked to her this week," Stewart said.

"Only for a few minutes at a time, in the evening, or when I've stopped in the bistro to pick something up," I said.

"Are you two ever going to get married?" Stewart asked.

I sighed. "I hope so, but so far Helen Louise isn't ready. We have a lot of things to talk over, like where we'll live. Her house or my house, for example. Whether she'll keep her hours at the bistro down so we can have more time together when I'm not working. Things like that."

"I'd hate not to see you two get married, if that's what you really want," Stewart said.

"Me, too, but things aren't so bad this way," I said. "We love each other, and we'll work it out eventually." I didn't want to discuss it any further.

Stewart must have picked up on the note

of finality in my tone because he let the subject drop.

We talked of various things while I finished my dinner, and then Stewart said he was heading upstairs to watch television after he took Dante out to the backyard for a brief run.

"I'll bid you good night, then." I took my plate and utensils to the sink to rinse. "Haskell ought to be home soon."

"Good night," Stewart said. "Come on, Dante. Walkies."

Dante yipped with excitement and trotted after Stewart.

"No, Ramses, you can't go with them. Come back here." For once he actually minded me, stopping in midrun to turn around and return to my side. "Good boy, Ramses." I rubbed his head, and he purred. Diesel did not look amused at this attention to his little brother. He turned and sat with his back to us.

"Let's go watch television, too." Ramses followed me, and I didn't look to see whether Diesel did. When we reached the den, however, Diesel pushed past me and climbed onto the sofa. I went to my recliner and picked up the remote. Before I could even settle myself in the recliner, Ramses scrambled up onto my lap, circled around three times, and then curled up and tucked his head in.

The television was still set to the station with the old programs, and I relaxed and let my mind drift while I watched the antics of various old-time sitcom stars.

I worried about the motives of the impostor Zwake. What was he up to? I couldn't rid myself of the uneasy feeling that mischief was afoot — mischief that would interfere with a successful performance on Saturday evening. I knew I was inclined to be a worrywart, as Laura labeled it, but past experience had taught me to trust these feelings. I wouldn't relax until the curtain came down at the end of the play on Saturday.

Thus far Lombardi had been the object of the prankster's tricks. They were all malicious, the third particularly so, because Lombardi's throat could have been damaged badly enough to keep him from performing. I gave a thought briefly to the understudy, Jared. Just how ambitious was he? I wondered.

I also wondered if Frank had considered the possibility that Jared could be the prankster. The motive was obvious in this case. He might have wanted to play the part so badly that he was willing to intimidate and injure Lombardi to keep him off the stage.

If Jared was the culprit, he was utterly ruthless. He hadn't achieved his goal yet, however. Would he try again? There was only the dress rehearsal remaining tomorrow afternoon, unless he somehow managed to get to Lombardi in his suite at the Farrington House.

I checked my watch. Surely Frank and Laura were home by now. I pulled out my phone and started to call. Then I put the phone down. I wasn't sure Frank and Laura would appreciate my *helpfulness* in this regard. They ought to know Jared well enough to decide whether he should have been considered a suspect in the pranks. *Yes, better to leave them alone,* I told myself. *Let them relax at home with baby Charlie.*

Determined not to obsess over the situation at the theater, I did my best to focus on the program currently on the screen. I'd seen it before, several times, but it was entertaining.

A few minutes later, Haskell startled me by walking into the den and hailing me.

"Sorry, Charlie," he said. "I thought you probably heard me calling you."

"No, but it's okay." I muted the volume on the television set. "What's up? Did something else happen at the theater?"

Haskell looked tired when he nodded. He glanced around for a place to sit and chose my desk chair. He leaned wearily back in it and regarded me somberly.

"Laura and Lombardi had another blowup right after you left to come home," he said. "I'm not sure what really started it, but it was probably Lombardi's fault."

"Oh, dear," I said. "I know Laura didn't react well. Did she?"

"No, she didn't," he replied. "Who could blame her? He seems to have it in for her for some reason. Anyway, they were going at it, yelling and carrying on, when Frank and I reached them in their dressing rooms. We made it to the door in time to hear Laura say she'd bash his head in if he kept behaving like an idiot."

FIFTEEN

All the next day in the office, while I tried to concentrate on the work at hand, I kept remembering what Haskell had shared with me when he returned from the theater. Laura would not follow through on her threat to bash Lombardi on the head. She was not a violent person, but I had little doubt she found the overbearing actor provoking enough to be tempted.

You have to stop worrying about this. It's a waste of energy. I told myself that several times throughout the day, but I didn't always pay attention when I gave myself excellent advice.

If Melba had been at work today, she would have no doubt provided distraction, because I could have queried her about her friend Katrinka. Melba had reconsidered her decision to return to work today. In a text earlier this morning, she told me she was simply too tired to face the thought of getting ready for work. I commiserated with her but told her she was doing the best thing for herself.

The building was quiet today with Melba out. Our mutual boss, Andrea Taylor, spent most of the day elsewhere on campus in various meetings. Knowing what Andrea's schedule was like reinforced the decision I had made not to accept the offer for the job last year. The thought of spending so much of my life in meetings didn't appeal to me, but that was an everyday part of the life of a library director on a college campus.

I had talked to Laura this morning to find out how they were doing, and she assured me everything was fine. She had two classes this morning, but after that, she was free to rest and get ready for the dress rehearsal tonight.

Before I could ask her whether she wanted me there, she said, "You know, Dad, you've been really good all week, coming to rehearsals, but I don't think you have to be there tonight. The dress rehearsal will probably be a disaster, but that means the performance tomorrow will be great. I'd rather you see that, okay?"

I thought she seemed a little eager to keep me away from tonight's rehearsal, but I let it pass without comment. I did wonder, however, if she had been conferring with her brother about my tendency to poke my nose in. I wouldn't put it past them to decide that I needed to be kept out of the loop so I couldn't get myself — or them — in trouble. After my foolish behavior in the last murder case, I guess I couldn't really blame them.

"That's fine, sweetheart," I said, my tone bland. "I'm ready for a relaxing afternoon at home with my boys. Ramses has been missing me."

"Even with Azalea there every day?" Laura asked.

"Yes," I said. "He likes attention from me, too, especially after Azalea goes home."

"What if she decides to take him home with her over the weekend?"

Azalea sometimes did that. Ramses had a habit of sneaking into the bag she brought with her every day, in addition to a handbag. She tended to leave the bag in a conspicuous, easily reachable place on Fridays if she wanted to tempt Ramses into it. I didn't mind her taking him home occasionally, but I wasn't ready to give him up completely.

"That will be fine," I said. "She takes good care of him."

"I don't want you to feel left out." Laura sounded uncertain all of a sudden.

"I'm okay, sweetheart," I said. "Don't worry about me. You focus on your performance. I'm expecting you to give me a Tony winner tomorrow night."

She laughed at that. "Okay, Dad, it's a deal. Love you."

"I love you, too. Now go." I heard her chuckle before I ended the call.

I swiveled my chair to talk to Diesel, perched in the window embrasure behind my desk. "We're not going to rehearsal this afternoon, buddy. We're going to go home instead after work. How does that sound?"

I knew he recognized the word *home,* and he warbled happily. As much as he loved Laura, he found the theater confusing, I knew, and Laura had little time to interact with him there. We would both be better off resting at home.

When three o'clock came, I shut down my computer and prepared to leave. "Come on, boy," I said. Diesel slid out of the window onto the floor and led me to the door. I had driven today, in anticipation of going to the dress rehearsal; otherwise we could have walked home. The spring afternoon was pleasantly sunny, with a light breeze. I was tempted to walk Diesel home and then walk back to retrieve the car, simply to spend some time outside in the fresh air.

I decided against it, however, and was glad I did when we reached home and I took Diesel into the kitchen. After greeting Azalea and Ramses, and giving the latter the attention he wanted, I decided to go to the den, lie back in my recliner, and nap. I knew Azalea would call when dinner was ready, and I told her where I would be.

Azalea nodded. "You go rest. You're looking a little peaked today."

I didn't think I looked any such thing, but I didn't stick around to argue. I headed for the den and got comfortable. Ramses stayed with Azalea — she was cooking, after all, and a starving kitten never knew when treats might appear — but Diesel came with me and stretched out on the sofa. Before long, I think we both fell asleep.

Azalea woke me for dinner over an hour later, and I ate alone. Stewart was out somewhere, and Haskell was still at dress rehearsal, I presumed. I itched to know how things were going and briefly considered driving over to have a sneak peek, but I talked myself out of it.

Later that evening, I had a brief chat with an exhausted Helen Louise. I decided not to burden her with the latest goings-on surrounding the play. Time enough for that later. We talked of other things before bidding each other good night.

During the day on Saturday, I heard nothing about dress rehearsal the night before. Haskell got called out early that morning to assist with a situation in a rural part of the county, and I didn't see him again until that evening when he and Stewart attended the play.

Henry was still on vacation, and Helen Louise didn't have anyone to cover for him and herself, so she was going to miss the play tonight. I was disappointed that she couldn't come, but she had no choice. After she had finally prevailed upon Henry to take his overdue vacation, she couldn't cavil at the time he chose because she wanted to attend a play.

Azalea had taken Ramses home for the weekend, so I had to decide whether to find someone to stay with Diesel while I was attending the play, or leave him by himself. I finally came to the conclusion that he would be fine by himself for a few hours this evening. I set the television in the den to an animal channel that always captured his attention and made sure he had fresh water and food. I explained the situation to him, and he didn't make a fuss when I left for the theater. I would see Sean, Alex, Stewart, and Haskell there. I thought their seats were near mine, but I didn't know for sure.

I consoled myself, and partly assuaged my feelings of guilt by reminding myself how smart he was. He wouldn't do anything foolish and get himself in trouble while I was gone. He would settle down happily with the television and probably go to sleep.

I drove to the performing arts center on the Athena campus and found a parking spot. The performance started at seven thirty, and I arrived half an hour early. There were already quite a few cars in the parking lot, however.

In the lobby many people milled around, some standing in small clusters of three or four, chatting, and the steady buzz of conversation surrounded me. I wanted to go backstage to tell Laura to break a leg, but I thought it best that I leave her and Frank both to their preshow preparations. Instead I showed an usher my ticket and went to my seat.

Thanks to my inside connections, I had an aisle seat five rows back from the stage in the center section of the theater. I should be able to see all the action clearly. While I sat and played a few games of solitaire on my phone, I watched people trickle in. I spotted a number of people I knew both from the college and from the public library, where I volunteered once a week. The head of the public library, Teresa Farmer, waved at me, and I spotted Diesel's veterinarian, Dr. Romano, with a handsome young man in tow.

I felt a hand on my shoulder, and I looked up to see Miss An'gel standing over me.

"Good evening, Charlie," she said. "So nice to see you this evening. I'm sure you're looking forward to this as much as we are."

I stood to give her a quick peck on the cheek, and one also to Miss Dickce. Their ward, Benjy Stephens, dressed smartly in a dark suit, white shirt, and red tie, accompanied them. I greeted him with a handshake and a smile, and he inquired how I was doing.

These niceties finished, I discovered that the sisters and their ward had the seats next to me. Miss An'gel directed Miss Dickce to the fourth seat and Benjy to the third, while Miss An'gel herself took the seat next to me. Well used to submitting to Miss An'gel's directions, neither Miss Dickce nor Benjy demurred. They simply did as they were bid. Miss Dickce winked at me as she stepped past me into the row of seats, and I had to suppress a chuckle. I couldn't help but recall the little escapade we had shared recently, when we eavesdropped on a gossip-laden lunch between Melba and two of her friends.

As if I had conjured her up by thinking of her, Melba appeared at my side as I was preparing to resume my seat.

"Hi, Charlie," she said.

"How are you?" I asked. She looked a bit wan to me still, but her eyes danced with excitement.

"Over the cold, thank the Lord, but I don't have all my energy back yet." She glanced at her ticket. "This is my row, seat number five."

"Then you're right by Benjy," I said.

"Fine by me," Melba said. "I like having a handsome man at my side."

Benjy blushed when Miss Dickce repeated Melba's remark to him, but he rose gallantly to the occasion. "My pleasure, Miss Melba."

Miss An'gel and I chatted, while Miss Dickce and Melba chatted over poor Benjy, who looked a bit dazed by the flow of words between the two women.

I had to ask Miss An'gel if her friend from New York would be in attendance tonight, and she regretfully shook her head. "I really hoped she could make it, but she's simply too busy at the moment mounting a new production."

"That's too bad." Frank and Laura would

be disappointed, though I knew that they hadn't really believed the director would make it here to see the play.

I thought about telling Miss An'gel about the two Finnegan Zwakes and the acts of sabotage, but this was neither the place nor the time to go into it. I kept an eye out for both. I eventually spotted Dingelbach two rows down, near the center of the row, chatting with a taller, dark-haired man beside him.

The houselights flickered, then slowly dimmed. All attention focused on the stage. A hush fell over the audience, and after thirty seconds or so, the curtain began to rise. I had a thrill when I saw Laura in her costume, looking stunning and thoroughly composed.

Lombardi gazed into the audience blindly, as if he were contemplating serious matters. Then the dialogue began, and we were off. The first act moved swiftly, and the curtain came down on it even though it seemed only a few minutes had passed. The lights came up again, and people started stirring out of their seats for intermission.

Miss An'gel turned to me. "What an excellent play," she said with enthusiasm. "If the second act is as good as the first, this is bound to be a hit, don't you think?"

"Yes, I do," I said.

"Laura and Mr. Lombardi are terrific together, aren't they?" Miss An'gel continued. "They definitely have chemistry."

I agreed that they did. I was as puzzled by it as I was pleased. I hadn't seen this kind of connection between them before, but there was a synergy between them on the stage that fairly crackled. I had no idea of its source, but it was undeniably potent.

I excused myself to visit the restroom and had to wait in line for a bit, but I made it back to my seat a couple of minutes before the second-act curtain was due to come up. The Ducotes, Benjy, and Melba were already there, anticipating the resumption of the action.

The opening scene of this act filled me with sudden dread. This was the scene where Laura handed Lombardi the drink. I barely breathed when the curtain came up, and the play resumed. I felt the usual sense of déjà vu as I watched.

Then came the moment that frightened me. Laura handed the seated Lombardi his drink. He seemed to hesitate, then lifted it and drained it in one gulp.

At first he appeared to be fine, but then he began gasping for breath and collapsed. He fell out of the chair onto the stage and writhed for what seemed an eternity. Then he went still. The glass, released from his hand, rolled across the stage.

SIXTEEN

I watched in horror as Luke Lombardi's body twitched onstage. Unlike the rest of the audience, I knew that this was not supposed to happen. Laura stood frozen in horror, staring at Lombardi as he died right in front of her.

I scrambled out of my seat and headed immediately for the steps on one side of the stage. While the audience sat, unaware yet of the truth, waiting for something else to happen, I heard Frank yell at someone to bring the curtain down.

By the time I reached Laura onstage, the curtain had come down and Frank was kneeling by Lombardi's body. Laura turned with a sob into my arms, and I hugged her close to me.

"Is he?" I nodded at the body.

Frank looked ill. He nodded. "No pulse. I tried to revive him, but it was too late," he managed to get out. "Oh, my Lord, how could this happen?"

We both became aware of the rising noise of conversation from the audience. "You'd better go talk to them," I said.

Frank nodded and rose as others rushed onto the stage. "Has anyone called the police? Or an ambulance?" I asked.

The enterprising Jared raised his hand. "Yes, I did."

I nodded and continued to hold my daughter. We all heard Frank explain to the audience that there had been an unfortunate accident, and medical help had been summoned. If they would please remain in their seats, he would have further information for them in a few minutes.

Frank stepped through the curtains and pulled them shut behind him. "I hope that will keep them calm for a bit," he said in a low voice.

"The police and an ambulance should be here any minute, sir," Jared said promptly.

"Thank you," Frank said.

"What are we going to do, sir?" Jared asked. "Will the play go on?" He sounded hopeful.

"No." Frank's tone was curt. "I want you all to clear the stage right now, but stand by in the wings until the police and the ambulance arrive. I'm sure the police will have questions for us."

I couldn't help but wonder whether Jared was responsible for Lombardi's death. The young man seemed ghoulishly eager for the play to continue, with him taking over the role, no doubt. I shuddered. Surely the young man wasn't that insensitive?

Maybe he *was* that ambitious, however.

That was a disturbing thought to have about someone I knew nothing about. I'd had no chance to voice my suspicions about him to either Frank or Laura, and at the moment I had other concerns.

Laura's sobs had turned into sniffles, and she accepted my handkerchief with a watery smile. "I can't believe this happened, Dad. Right here onstage in front of all these people. It's horrible." The tears threatened again.

"Yes, it is horrible," I said, "but you didn't put the poison, whatever it was, in the glass. You didn't kill him, so don't start thinking you did."

Laura sniffled. "I know it, but I still can't help feeling guilty. The way I yelled at him this week. He made me so angry a couple of times, I think I could have bashed his head in. But not this. Never this."

"Hush now. I know that." I watched over her shoulder as the EMTs and a couple of

Athena police officers arrived. Chief Deputy Kanesha Berry of the county sheriff's department entered almost upon their heels. I figured Haskell must have called her. I glanced around and saw Haskell, in his suit and tie, heading toward his boss.

Later, in my memories of it, the next hour took on a nightmare tinge. After a brief conversation with the Athena police who responded to the call, Kanesha went out to address the audience. She explained that unfortunately Mr. Lombardi had had some kind of seizure and passed away. She asked for their patience while everything was taken care of and to please remain where they were for now.

There were murmurs of protest, but by and large, from what I heard, people were content — or too consumed by morbid curiosity — to want to leave before more details came their way.

I was allowed to take Laura to the green-room, where Frank and several of the cast members joined us. Frank sat on a sofa with an arm around Laura's shoulder, and the two of them spoke in undertones to each other. No longer needed to soothe my daughter, I had the leisure to survey the room.

It took me a moment to catch on to it,

but I finally realized that the student cast members kept throwing odd glances at Frank and Laura. The only one who didn't was Jared, who sat slightly apart from the others. They all no doubt knew about the scenes between the dead man and my daughter, the terrible outbursts when Laura had threatened her costar. Did they really think she had decided to kill him, and in such a public way? This idea disturbed me, but the more I watched them, the more I became convinced that I was right.

I knew one of them, if not all of them, would share this with the investigating officer. In this case, Kanesha Berry. I also knew that Kanesha would not arrest Laura on such slim evidence, but there was no doubt, in my mind, at least, that Laura would be considered the chief suspect by many.

As I had once before, I determined that I would do everything in my power to root out the killer and protect my daughter. Laura and Frank might get aggravated with me for poking my nose into this, but I wasn't about to stand by and let my daughter get blamed for something I knew she hadn't done. Lombardi had annoyed other people besides Laura. He had treated both Anton and Madame poorly. He had also stood in the way of an ambitious young actor, I was convinced. That Jared would think that taking over the lead role in this regional play was going to get him anywhere was ludicrous.

Unless, I thought, he had somehow heard about the Broadway director who might have been coming to see the play. That might have been the goad that pushed him into such a terrible deed. It was a horrible gamble, and as it turned out, the woman hadn't made it, but he might have thought the risk was worth it.

When I got the chance, I would share all this with Kanesha. She might not be happy with me, either, but she knew me well enough by now at least to hear me out. I had given her valuable help in the past that had led to convictions. She had no real reason to complain, I told myself somewhat complacently.

Time dragged by, and the atmosphere in the greenroom remained tense and uneasy. Every one of us fidgeted. The situation almost demanded it. The room was warm, and I got up to look for the control for the air-conditioning. Frank saw what I was doing and informed me irritably that the control was in the next room. He got up to see about it, but the police officer at the door wouldn't let him leave the room.

Haskell appeared about half an hour after we had moved to the room and asked Laura and Frank to go with him. He cast me a sympathetic glance but said nothing to me. I remained in the room with the young people. They whispered among themselves, and I caught them casting speculative glances my way. There wasn't much to look at in the room, other than reproductions of ugly paintings on the walls. Whoever had furnished this room was utterly devoid of taste or judgment, I decided.

Soon the actors began to be called out, one by one, with Jared being the first to leave the room. Finally, after an hour and a few minutes, I was alone in the room and started to get really peeved. I had been in the audience when Lombardi collapsed on-stage and died. Why was I being left in this stuffy, uncomfortable room till the last?

I had almost worked up the nerve to demand to be seen, or to be released, when Haskell entered the room and asked me to go with him.

"About time," I said testily.

"Sorry about that, Charlie," Haskell replied. "It couldn't be helped."

"I don't see why," I said, feeling argumentative. "Look, I know it's not your fault. I'm blaming your boss."

181

Haskell ignored that. "You know the routine."

"I do," I said. "I'm not going to answer any questions, though, until I get something to drink. That room was hot, and I'm thirsty." I knew I sounded like a petulant child, but I was tired and my head had begun to ache. I didn't think my demand for water was all that extreme.

Haskell stopped by a water fountain and gestured toward it. I drank my fill, and I started feeling better. The ache in my head began to recede, and my mood improved a little.

"Thanks. That really helped," I said.

Haskell nodded. "We're not unreasonable."

"I know, and I didn't mean to take out my irritation on you. This whole thing has got me upset."

"Understood," Haskell said as he ushered me back through the wings and onto the stage. The curtain was up again, and the audience had evidently been dismissed.

Someone had arranged several chairs in a semicircle at center stage, and Kanesha occupied a chair that faced the others. Frank and Laura sat next to each other at one end of the semicircle. Kanesha indicated that I should take the chair directly in front of her.

I did as she bade me and sat regarding her, waiting for her to begin the conversation. She looked me straight in the eye and said, "Good evening, Charlie. I can't say I'm happy about this situation."

"Good evening, Kanesha. I can't say I'm all that happy myself. It's not every day that I watch someone die right in front of me." As I made the semiflippant comment, the real horror of the situation finally hit me, and for a moment, I could hardly breathe. I had avoided until now thinking about the terrible death throes the man had suffered. I felt nauseated.

Laura must have noticed my distress, because she immediately came to sit next to me and slid her arm around my shoulders. She put her head close to mine and said into my ear, "I know, Dad. Just try to take deep breaths. One at a time."

Kanesha forbore to comment during this brief interlude. I gained control of myself and thanked Laura. She kissed my cheek before she returned to sit with her husband.

"Do you feel able to continue?" Kanesha asked, her tone softer than it had been.

"Yes," I said. "My apologies."

"I understand," she said. "Now, take your

time and tell me everything you observed after the second act curtain came up."

I nodded and took a minute to consider what I had seen. "I was focused on the stage like everyone else. I had already seen most of the play in rehearsal, so I knew what to expect." I paused, struck by a thought. Had Frank or Laura told Kanesha about what had happened during this same scene when Lombardi drank the doctored tea?

Was it my imagination, or was Kanesha watching me more intently than usual?

I had paused too long, and I hurried into speech. "Anyway, I was watching both actors. I thought Lombardi hesitated briefly before he drank. Then he tossed the drink back, and for a moment, he seemed okay. Then he collapsed and thrashed about a bit onstage. I got up and ran to the side of the stage to the steps so I could get to Laura. I saw how terrified she was."

Kanesha consulted her notebook, and I waited. She looked up. "You were present on the previous occasion when a similar incident occurred during the rehearsal of this same scene. Is that correct?"

"Yes, I was." What was she after?

"How was this scene different?" she asked.

"Other than the obvious things, like this being the actual performance, and the actors all being in costume and makeup, the only thing different was that brief hesitation before Lombardi drank. He didn't do that in the rehearsal I saw. I didn't attend the dress rehearsal last night. Did he do it then?"

"According to witnesses, he did," Kanesha said. "Did you happen to see his expression right after he downed the drink?"

I frowned, trying to recall. Before I could answer, Anton rushed onto the stage and halted everything. Wild-eyed, sobbing, he pointed a shaky finger at Laura.

"*Meurtrière!* She is the one. She killed *mon maître.*"

SEVENTEEN

For a moment we all stared at the disheveled, quivering Anton. He continued to point at Laura and broke into a stream of French.

Haskell stepped forward with another deputy and took Anton by the arms and led him away on Kanesha's instruction. "I'll talk to him when you've got him calmed down."

Even she appeared slightly shaken by the outburst from the raving Frenchman. Her tone showed no evidence of it, however, when she spoke. "That was Anton du Jardin, I gather. He was Mr. Lombardi's dresser. Is that the correct term?"

"Yes, it is," Frank said. "Valet, really. Looks after the actor's clothes and helps him dress and get ready to go onstage." He had one arm around Laura's shoulder, and I watched my daughter with concern. She appeared really shaken by Anton's ravings.

"Thank you," Kanesha said. "Now, Charlie, do you have anything to add to what you've told me about tonight?"

I wanted to talk to her about Jared — I really ought to find out the young man's surname, I realized — but not until I'd had a chance to discuss him with Frank and Laura first. I didn't want to accuse him out of hand.

"No, not that I can think of at the moment," I said.

Her tone was dry when she replied, "I'm sure you'll let me know if you think of anything else." She closed her notebook. "You're all free to go now. I will have more questions for you tomorrow, however."

"Thank you." I rose from my chair. "This has been a terrible thing for everyone concerned."

I shepherded Laura and Frank in front of me, and I followed them to Laura's dressing room while she collected her purse and a jacket. She had removed her stage makeup at some point, but her eyes were still a bit red and strained-looking. Frank appeared ready to fall into bed at any moment.

"How about I take you both home?" I asked. "Neither one of you needs to be driving tonight."

Frank nodded. "Thank you. Everything is crashing in on both of us, I think."

"Come on, then," I said.

We made slow but steady progress out of the theater and to the parking lot. I had them home less than ten minutes later, and I told them I wouldn't come in. "Go to bed," I said. "Try to rest, and sleep late in the morning."

"Thanks, Dad." Laura kissed me before she slid out of the front seat. Frank squeezed my shoulder before he exited the backseat.

I watched them until they were inside the house. My heart hurt for them. They had both put so much time and physical and creative energy into this production, and to see it ruined like this pained me deeply.

I drove on home, thinking about the playwright. I hadn't seen him again after I spotted him in the audience before the first curtain went up. I imagined he was pretty shaken up, too. The murderer had, in a sense, profaned Dingelbach's work by using it as a vehicle for a cold-blooded, merciless killing.

Stewart had made it home an hour ago, I was relieved to find. He was in the kitchen with Diesel and Dante. He had a magazine spread open on the table. He closed it and got up to give me a quick hug.

"How are you?" he asked.

"Exhausted and horrified, I think." I sank

into my chair and let my head rest in my hands. I felt Diesel's paw on my leg, and I sat up again. I rubbed his head to soothe him.

"I'm okay, boy. Don't worry," I said.

"How about some hot tea? Or maybe a shot of brandy?" Stewart asked. "I had a couple of shots when I got home." He indicated the bottle on the table.

"Brandy sounds good, actually," I said. "Thanks."

Stewart poured brandy into an empty glass and handed it to me. I sipped at it and felt the warmth begin to spread. Stewart waited in silence until I finished.

"More?" he asked.

"No, I think that's enough. I do feel better. Thanks."

"Do you want to talk about it?"

I hesitated. "It was horrible to watch him die like that. It felt almost" — I searched for the word — "*obscene* to sit there and watch it like a perverted voyeur."

"You knew it for what it was, I guess," Stewart said. "I think Haskell did, too, but I didn't. The rest of the audience didn't, either, so it was several minutes before the horror set in for us."

A thought I had been pushing ruthlessly to the back of my mind finally broke

189

through, and I thought I would faint when it did.

"What is it?" Stewart half-rose from his chair.

I waved him back. "Laura." My breath felt constricted. "Laura was supposed to take a drink, too, from that same bottle. Oh, dear Lord, she could have died just like Lombardi."

With that, I surrendered to the terror, and the sobs came. The idea of losing my beautiful daughter terrified me, and the emotions rushed through me. Stewart came and knelt beside me. He placed his arms around me and rocked me while I cried. I knew Diesel was upset to see me this way, but in my misery, I couldn't help it.

Finally, the storm began to abate. I had no idea how long I'd been crying. My eyes felt swollen, and my head ached abominably. Stewart released me, and I heard the faucet running. He came back to me with a cold, wet cloth, and I pressed it to my face. The cold felt so soothing.

Stewart knelt again beside me, but this time he comforted my distraught feline. "It's okay, Diesel. Daddy is going to be fine." The cat mewed anxiously, and I took the cloth away from my face. I held my arms open, and Diesel pulled away from Stewart to climb into my lap. I held him close, and he rubbed his head against my face.

Stewart still hovered beside us both, and Dante danced around his legs. I looked up at Stewart. I thanked him again, and he squeezed my shoulder. For the first time I realized he had been crying, too.

"I think I'm going up to bed," I said. "I'm worn out."

"I'll go up, too," Stewart said. "Come on, Dante, bedtime."

I let go of Diesel, and he climbed down from my lap. I turned off all the lights in the kitchen except the one that we always left on. Stewart and Dante waited for us at the foot of the stairs, and Stewart insisted that I precede him. I figured he was worried I might collapse again.

Diesel and I made it safely up the stairs, and Stewart came to the door of my bedroom with me. "Is there anything you need, anything I can do for you?"

"No, I'm okay now," I said. "If I should need you during the night, I'll let you know." I hugged him and bade him good night.

Wearily I stripped off my clothes, not bothering to hang up my suit jacket and pants. I threw them across a chair and then went to the bathroom to wash my face again. When I came back into the bedroom, Diesel was already on the bed, his head on his pillow.

He watched me closely until I was in bed beside him. I made myself comfortable, then switched off the light. I stroked Diesel and concentrated on relaxing both my body and my mind. I soon drifted into a doze, and that was the last I remembered until I awoke the next morning.

I sat up on the side of the bed and looked for my phone. I had to think about what I had done with it. I hadn't done anything, I realized, except leave it in my jacket. I retrieved the phone and checked the time. Almost eight a.m. Then I looked for messages. I had missed a call from Helen Louise. I frowned. I hadn't heard the phone.

I had set it on silent last night before the play started, I remembered. I would call Helen Louise later and apologize, but even had the ringer been on, I might not have surfaced from sleep. I had slept so soundly, I felt a bit of a sleep hangover this morning. I glanced over at Diesel's side of the bed. Empty. He was probably downstairs eating his breakfast.

Back to the phone. No messages from my children, either. I wanted to call and check on Frank and Laura, but I decided to wait until nine. Surely they'd be up by then. Baby Charlie would get them up. Then I remembered that Charlie had spent the night at Sean's house, under the care of Cherelle, the nanny, while Sean and Alex attended the play.

I had a hot shower before I went down for breakfast, and I felt much revived after the shower. Thoughts about Lombardi's death and Laura's miraculous escape haunted me, but I tried to keep them from overwhelming me. I smelled coffee and heard voices when I was halfway down the stairs.

Haskell and Stewart sat drinking coffee, and Frank was with them. Diesel sat beside Frank's chair and didn't leave his side when he saw me. He must have decided that Frank needed comforting.

"Good morning." I went to the counter to pour myself some coffee, added cream and sugar, then carried it to the table. "How is everyone this morning?"

Haskell and Frank both looked tired, and I feared Frank had suffered a sleepless night. Haskell had likely not made it home until the early hours of the morning. Stewart looked pretty chipper, though.

"Doing fine," Haskell said.

Frank shrugged. "Didn't get much sleep last night." He locked eyes with me. "I'm

193

sure you understand why."

I felt that jab of fear again. I nodded. "How is Laura?"

"She took something to help her sleep. I think she had a better night than I did," Frank said. "Thank the Lord. She's busy this morning with Charlie, and Alex is there with Rosie. I decided to clear out for a while, let them talk and play with the kids. That's the best therapy right now for Laura."

"Amen," I replied.

Frank looked at me again. "I've been over it and over it countless times since last night. I still can't figure out when, or how, someone was able to put that poison in the bottle."

"If it was in the bottle, then someone had to be able to put it there," Stewart said. "Where was the bottle kept?"

"In a cupboard in the prop room," Frank said.

"Was the prop room locked?" Stewart said.

"Yes, at all times, except when the prop manager or his assistant went in to retrieve something or put something back," Frank replied. "They both have keys, and I have one. There isn't another one. We're responsible for the keys during the run of the play, including all rehearsals and performances. When we're done, we have to return them to the custodian's office."

"You can't rule out the existence of another key, though, can you?" I asked.

"No, I can't," Frank said, "but I think it's unlikely, given the system in place."

"Is the building kept locked when it's not in use?" Haskell asked.

Frank shrugged. "I think so, but I don't know for sure."

Haskell looked at me.

"What about while it's in use?" I asked. "Which doors are unlocked?"

"The front doors, of course, and one side door off the stage," Frank said.

"I found one of the back doors unlocked on Tuesday," I said. "That could be significant. Someone unlocked that door, most likely from inside."

Haskell nodded in confirmation.

"I don't like the sound of that," Frank said.

"I don't, either," I replied. "But I think we have to consider the possibility that the killer is familiar with the building, or else he, or she, is working with someone who is."

EIGHTEEN

Frank stared hard at me. I could see he was considering what I had said.

"How well do you know the students in your cast and crew?" Stewart asked.

Frank shifted in his chair. "Pretty well. They're all juniors and seniors, except for one, Jared Eckworth. He's a sophomore. Really talented kid." He shrugged. "I don't know him well, but he's in one of Laura's classes this semester. History of the Theater, I think."

Jared Eckworth. "Is he the only Jared in the group?" I asked.

Frank nodded. "Why do you ask?"

"I saw Jared when he took Lombardi's place, remember? He's talented, as you say. I wanted to be sure it was the same young man. I didn't know his last name."

Frank appeared satisfied with my explanation. I didn't want to discuss my concerns about Jared in front of Haskell. Not that I didn't trust him, but I thought I ought to talk to Frank and Laura first before I shared my suspicions with an officer of the law. Laura might be able to allay those suspicions if she had a deeper acquaintance with the young man.

Haskell got up from the table and set his coffee mug in the sink. "I'm going upstairs for a shower," he said. "Frank, Charlie, I'm sure I'll be seeing you sometime later today."

Stewart looked after him anxiously, I thought. "He's really tired. I wish he had time to get more sleep, but he's got to be back at the sheriff's department at nine." He turned to me. "Charlie, can I fix you anything for breakfast? Frank, what about you?"

Frank shook his head.

"I'm fine," I said. "I'm not ready to eat for a bit yet. You go on up to Haskell."

"Okay, thanks." Stewart scooped up his dog and carried him out of the kitchen.

I turned to my son-in-law and eyed him with sympathy. "I'd like to talk to you, but it can wait. I think you should go back home and try to sleep."

"No, every time I fall asleep, I have the same nightmare." He looked away from me. "I'm sure you know what it is."

I felt guilty for having slept through the

night, knowing that he had been tortured so.

"Yes, I know," I said. "But thank the merciful Lord, it didn't happen." I hesitated. "I have to ask, though, why didn't she drink when he did?"

"Superstition," Frank said. "At least, I think that's what it was. The first time we rehearsed it, she drank at the same time, and he swallowed that horrible, caustic liquid." He looked ill for a moment. "At the dress rehearsal, she hesitated — I'm not sure why — and everything was fine. I believe she thought that if she waited to drink after him last night, everything would be fine again."

"Did Kanesha ask you that?"

"Yes, she did, and I told her the same thing," Frank said. "Laura admitted it but really couldn't explain it. Kanesha jumped on that and grilled Laura really hard about it." He rubbed his forehead. "I know it looks bad, given what happened, but that's all it was. Superstition."

"Kanesha didn't believe it?" I asked.

"She didn't act like she did," Frank replied. "If Laura had poisoned Luke, then of course Laura wouldn't have drunk the same stuff she had just given him. I could tell Kanesha thought that was suspicious."

"I can't believe she thinks Laura is a murderer," I said, aghast.

"I don't think she really does believe it." Frank surprised me. "But she has to cover every possibility. You know that. The students obviously told Kanesha about the big flare-up between Laura and Luke, and Kanesha had to question her. But Kanesha knows Laura wouldn't kill somebody."

"I sure hope not." What was I going to say to Kanesha when I saw her next? I wasn't happy about this, though I understood Frank's points.

"What happened to the bottle from last night?" I asked.

"I'm not sure. I thought maybe Haskell grabbed it, but he says he didn't. Maybe one of the other officers took possession of it. Kanesha will know."

If the bottle had disappeared, it meant that the killer or his accomplice had been onstage after Lombardi collapsed and died. Who had been on the stage? I tried to recall the scene, but I hadn't been paying much attention to anyone other than Laura, Frank, and Lombardi.

Jared. The name popped into my consciousness. Jared Eckworth had been onstage. I decided it was time to talk to Frank about the young man, now that Haskell had left the room.

"Frank, about Jared Eckworth," I said.

"Let me get another cup of coffee," Frank said.

I waited until he was seated again and sipping at his coffee. "About Jared."

"I don't know that I can tell you much about him," Frank said.

"Yes, I know. You said he was one of Laura's students, but you had to work with him as Lombardi's understudy. You must have formed some impressions of him," I said.

"Yes," Frank said. "He's a hard worker, a lot of talent, still rough around the edges. Eager to do well. I won't be surprised if he drops out of school at some point to head to either New York or L.A."

"Ambitious," I said, and Frank nodded.

"Ruthless?" I asked.

Frank's eyes narrowed. "What are you getting at, Charlie?"

"Those pranks, at least the first two," I said. "Scaring Lombardi and then potentially damaging his voice so he couldn't go on. Would a ruthless understudy pull things like that in order to take the principal's place?"

Frank shifted uncomfortably in his chair. "I hate to admit this, but I did wonder the same thing after the second incident."

"Did you discuss it with Laura?"

"I mentioned it," Frank said, "and she told me not to be ridiculous. She seems fond of Jared, thinks he's bright and promising."

"Do you remember what he said when we were all onstage with the body?"

Frank looked puzzled. "No. I guess I was too much in shock to notice anything except poor Luke. What did Jared say?"

"I don't remember the exact words," I said. "The gist of it was, he wanted to know if the play would go on last night after Lombardi's body was removed from the stage. That seemed really cold, not to say heartless, to me."

"Are you sure you heard him right?" Frank's shock was all too obvious. "That's hard to believe. He seems like a nice kid."

"Yes, I heard him right. He's a little too eager, if you ask me," I replied. "That's what made me wonder if he wasn't responsible for the first two pranks."

"I can see that he might have done those two," Frank said. "But deliberate murder? That's too much."

"He didn't seem all that bothered by a corpse on the stage," I said. "That wasn't natural, at least to me."

"I just can't see him as a cold-blooded killer," Frank said. "I've never seen any signs of psychopathic behavior in him, and I do know the signs. I worked with an actor once who was an out-and-out psychopath. Jared hasn't come across that way to me, not once."

Frank's certainty shook my own. I realized I had seized on Jared as the culprit a little too eagerly.

"I trust your instincts," I said. "I still think he has to be considered, though. His wanting to go on after Lombardi collapsed and died simply doesn't seem normal to me."

"No, to me, either, but then I'm a dozen years older than Jared," Frank said. "He's young for his age in some ways. I don't know if he's ever even seen a dead person before. The reality of the situation might not have hit him until later."

"True," I said. "I didn't say anything about this last night to Kanesha, because I wanted to talk to you and Laura first. I think Kanesha has to know what he said, however. If I don't tell her, I imagine another cast member or one of the stagehands probably will."

"Okay," Frank said. "You're right. I know Kanesha will handle the whole thing fairly." He pushed himself up from the table.

"Guess I'll head back home now. I'll talk to Laura about Jared for you."

"Thanks." I followed him to the front door, along with Diesel. Frank bent slightly to pat Diesel on the head. "Try to get some rest."

Frank nodded. "I will. I'm so dang tired right now."

I watched him until he was in his car and driving away. Then I retrieved the Sunday paper from the yard and went back inside. Diesel kept pace with me to the kitchen.

I poured myself more coffee and sat to open the paper. The front doorbell rang. I had a feeling I knew who it was, and I groaned. I wasn't ready for this, but I knew there was no putting it off.

As expected, I found Kanesha Berry on the front doorstep.

"Good morning," she said. "I hope I didn't wake you, but I have questions for you, and I need the answers."

"You didn't wake me." I stood aside and waved her in. "I think there's enough coffee in the pot for a cup, if you want it, or I can make some more."

"I'm fine. Thanks." She strode ahead of me into the kitchen.

Diesel had meowed at her, his way of saying hello, but she appeared too preoccupied to notice. I resumed my place at the table, and Diesel stretched out on the floor beside my chair.

"What do you want to ask?" I debated whether to confront her over her stiff questioning of my daughter, but decided to wait.

Kanesha had pulled out her notebook and laid it on the table, but she didn't consult it.

"I want to know what it was you were holding back last night." Her tone was not accusatory, simply matter-of-fact.

I sometimes wished she didn't know me so well, because she had learned to read me too easily. I stared into my coffee, trying to organize my thoughts. This was happening sooner than I expected, and I had wanted more time to think about what Frank and I discussed.

"Well?" Kanesha prompted me.

"Gathering my thoughts," I said. "There are a couple of things. Has anyone told you about the incident with the really hot pepper in the bottle during one of the rehearsals?"

Kanesha nodded. "Yes, I heard about it. Go on."

"What I didn't tell you last night was a statement I heard made by one of the student actors. Lombardi's understudy, in fact."

"Jared Eckworth." Kanesha nodded.

"Yes, Jared," I replied. "We were standing there around Lombardi's dead body, and Jared wanted to know if the play could go on once the body was cleared from the stage."

"Thank you," Kanesha said. "That corroborates what one of the other students said. Why didn't you tell me this last night?"

"I don't know the young man," I said, "but Frank and Laura do. I wanted to find out more about him, that's all."

Kanesha didn't look impressed by this, and I supposed I couldn't blame her. It sounded lame now, even to me.

"Has anyone told you about the other prank aimed at Lombardi?" I asked.

"Yes," Kanesha said. "Both pretty nasty, especially since Lombardi was known to have a fear of snakes. But the second one was worse." She paused for a moment. "Do you think Eckworth is the prankster?"

I squirmed a little in my chair. "I think he's certainly a good possibility. He's talented. He took Lombardi's place after the second prank, during the run-through, and he was excellent."

"He'd have to be pretty dang ruthless to

pull stunts like that," Kanesha said. "Do you think he'd murder a man in cold blood in order to take his place onstage?"

"I don't know. I don't know the young man. Frank was here this morning, and I talked to him about it. Frank doesn't think Eckworth is capable of it. Frank says he knows psychopathic behavior when he sees it, having worked with an actor once who was a psychopath."

Kanesha did not appear moved by Frank's assessment. "Seems like an extreme tactic, just for a college play."

I realized then that she didn't know about Miss An'gel's ruse to keep Lombardi in line. If she did, she was being cagey about it.

"The stakes could have been considerably higher than a simple college play." I told her about Miss An'gel's stratagem. "It really worked. Lombardi behaved well, most of the time. Miss An'gel was seated next to me last night in the theater, and she told me she really had invited her friend down, but the woman had too many commitments."

"You think word of this somehow leaked to the rest of the cast, and this was the impetus for the pranks and, ultimately, the murder? So the killer could perform for this director?"

I nodded. "It sounds crazy, I know, but

you've dealt with people who will stop at nothing to get what they want."

"I have," Kanesha said. "And so have you. But this has too many *ifs* in it. *If* the woman came to the play, *if* she was impressed by Eckworth, *if* she offered to make him a star on Broadway, and so on."

"I know," I said. "Crazy, right? But we both know people have been motivated by nuttier reasons."

"I'll be talking to Eckworth again, along with all the students and the stagehands. Custodial staff, too. One of them might have seen something."

"Have you heard about the fake play-wright?"

Kanesha looked intrigued. "No, I haven't. Tell me."

Starting with his appearance at the reception last Saturday night, I gave her a run-down on my interactions and sightings of the fake Finnegan Zwake. Then I told her about the appearance of the authentic one, and she jotted down his name in her note-book.

"I remember his father," she said. "Had Frank and Laura previously met the impostor before the rehearsals began?"

I frowned, thinking. "I believe so, but you'll have to ask them. Frank seemed to know him."

"But none of you had met the real one, Dingelbach."

"No, I certainly hadn't, though I took a class from his father, eons ago," I said.

"Can you give me a description of the impostor?"

"Tall, lanky, fiery-red hair, a big mop of it, and a long, thick mustache to match."

Kanesha's eyebrows shot up as I talked. "That explains what one of the grounds-keepers found near the performing arts building early this morning," she said. "A red wig and what he thought was a big caterpillar. A fake mustache."

NINETEEN

"I guess I should have figured out that he was wearing some sort of disguise," I said, chagrined. "That bush of hair and that mustache distracted me a bit, but what I really puzzled over was the name, Finnegan Zwake."

"It's obviously taken from James Joyce," Kanesha said. "What's the puzzle?"

I explained about the series of young adult novels whose main character had that name.

"Interesting, but I'm not sure I attach any particular significance to it," Kanesha said. "What I want to know is whether there is any connection between the impostor and Dingelbach. Did the impostor seem to know anything about the play?"

I had to cast back over the conversations with Zwake that I had been a party to before I could respond. "In a way, yes, but also in a way, no. He never said anything that showed knowledge of the plot of the play.

He made some comments to Lombardi about the character." I related the incident, and Kanesha nodded.

"I see what you mean. That statement about the character could apply to the lead in almost any play of substance," she said.

"What was the point of it all?" I asked. "Surely he had to know he'd be found out eventually, when the real Zwake turned up."

"It allowed him to get close to Lombardi," Kanesha said. "And he could show up at rehearsals and get backstage. No one would have thought much about it."

"No, probably not," I said. "Do you think he's a viable suspect?"

"Definitely," Kanesha said. "Until I find out who he really is, he's going to remain at the top of my list."

"I think you're right."

"Can you recall any distinguishing features, other than the hair and mustache?" Kanesha held her pen, ready to jot down whatever I said.

"No," I said. "Nothing that I can think of. But you ought to talk to Helen Louise. She was with me. She might have noticed something. Other people saw him at the party, too."

"We're working on getting the guest list for the reception," Kanesha said. "Once we have it, we'll start talking to everyone who was there."

"Routine police work," I said, thankful I didn't have to go through all that tedium.

Kanesha nodded. "It pays off most of the time."

"Miss An'gel and Miss Dickce came to the reception," I said. "You know how sharp-eyed they are."

"I've already talked to Miss An'gel," Kanesha said. "Last night, and again this morning."

"She didn't tell you about the ruse she concocted?" I asked.

"No, she didn't." Kanesha sounded the tiniest bit peeved about that.

"I imagine she had other things on her mind," I said.

"Perhaps."

I would have loved to be a fly on the wall during Kanesha's next conversation with Miss An'gel. While Kanesha was respectful to her elders — except occasionally to her own mother — she also was a hardened investigator who didn't tolerate omission or evasion lightly.

"Is there anything else?" I asked.

"No, that's it for now."

"Then I have a question for you," I said. "Do you *seriously* think that my daughter killed Lombardi?"

Kanesha fixed me with a hard stare. "You know I have to consider all the potential suspects, and even if you don't like it, Laura is a suspect. And a good one."

"My daughter could have died along with Lombardi last night," I said, my anger suddenly hitting me. "Thank the Lord she didn't drink that stuff. But you can't think she's a murderer because she didn't drink along with Lombardi."

Kanesha stared at me, eyes narrowed. Then she sighed, and her tensed shoulders dropped. "Look, I personally don't think Laura is guilty, all right? But I can't appear to give anyone preferential treatment. Until I know what the killer used, and how it got into that tea, I have to suspect everyone. Understood?"

I nodded, albeit reluctantly.

Kanesha stood and picked up her notebook. "I'll be in touch. Don't bother to see me out," she added when I pushed back my chair. She walked out of the kitchen, and I heard the front door open and close a few seconds later. Kanesha always closed a door firmly and audibly.

While I prepared my breakfast of bacon, scrambled eggs, and toast, I thought about the impostor Zwake. I kept trying to focus on his face, but mostly what I saw was the red hair and the mustache. What color were his eyes? Green? Hazel? I couldn't remember.

He was tall, perhaps several inches taller than I was at six one. What was the natural color of his hair? Either blond or brown, I guessed, and he would be clean-shaven; otherwise he wouldn't have worn the fake mustache.

I almost let my eggs burn because I was so distracted by the impostor's physical characteristics. Recalled to attention, I finished cooking and set my food on the table.

Diesel meowed hopefully at me when I sat. "Yes," I told him, "I cooked extra bacon so you could have a little." One slice only, but doled out in small pieces. "And a bite of egg if you're really good."

He warbled, and I took that to mean he really wanted the bite of egg. We ate in companionable silence, and Diesel didn't pester me for his tidbits, waiting patiently for me to offer them before he nearly bit my fingers off accepting them. I figured he might have picked that habit up from Dante. "Take it easy, boy."

At the moment I couldn't figure out any way to track down the impostor on my own.

That was best left to Kanesha and her people. Kanesha considered him the chief suspect, for now. That meant she and her team would put a lot of effort into finding him, and I had little doubt she would turn him up, unless he had fled Athena for good.

I would be on the lookout, of course, in case I spotted anyone who reminded me of him, but for now, there was at least one other suspect to consider. Jared Eckworth. Though Frank didn't seem to think the student actor was capable of murder, I decided it would be remiss of any investigator to count him out completely.

For example, what if he had played the two pranks? He might have hoped to knock Lombardi out of the performance, but not necessarily kill him. The actual killer could have been someone else who hoped that, when the identity of the prankster was established, that person would naturally be considered the chief suspect. So the killer had copied the second prank, but this time, the contents of the bottle were lethal.

My anger grew whenever I thought about that murderous act. Laura could easily have been a victim. I felt angry enough to commit murder myself right then. I felt my blood pressure rise until my head nearly vibrated from the throbbing.

My rational side began to assert itself, reminding me that causing a stroke or a heart attack wasn't the solution to anything. I forced myself to relax and take measured breaths until the throbbing eased considerably. I got up and filled a glass with cold water from the fridge and drank it down. That helped.

All during this interlude, Diesel had watched me but hadn't uttered a sound. When I sat again, he put both front paws in my lap and butted my stomach with his head. I allowed him to climb into my lap and stroked his back until we both felt better.

I urged Diesel gently from my lap and got up to take care of the breakfast dishes. Once I had finished with them, I went back upstairs to shower and dress. Today was the day for our weekly family get-together, but given what had happened yesterday, I wasn't sure we would all be dining together.

Refreshed by the shower, I followed Diesel downstairs to the kitchen, where I found Stewart busy with preparations for the noon meal. "Hello again," I said, and Stewart turned to acknowledge my greeting with a smile.

"Have you talked to anyone this morning?" I asked. "Other than Frank, that is. I wasn't sure if everyone would be in the mood after last night."

"Frank told Haskell and me this morning that he and Laura would be here, with the baby, of course. I called Sean about twenty minutes ago, and he said they'd be here, too. I left it to you to call Helen Louise," he said.

Pleased with this news, I pulled out my cell phone and checked the time. A little after nine thirty, so Helen Louise ought to be up. I waited, but the call went to voice mail. *Probably in the shower,* I thought, and put my phone on the table.

"She's not answering at the moment," I said. "Is there anything I can do to help?"

"How about peeling those potatoes by the sink?" Stewart pointed with his elbow while he continued whatever he was doing at the stove.

"Sure." I found the potato peeler and set to work. Stewart had washed eleven good-sized potatoes, and I peeled five of them before I decided to take a break and try Helen Louise again.

This time she answered. "Good morning, love. How are you?" she asked.

"Doing pretty good." I wasn't going to tell her about last night until I could do so in person. "Lunch is set for noon, as usual. I hope you're going to be here."

She laughed. "Of course I will. Where else would I be? I'll bring dessert."

"Well, if you didn't, there might be complaints." No one made chocolate desserts like Helen Louise did.

"I just got out of the shower," she said. "I'm going to have some coffee. Then I'll get dressed and be there by eleven, probably."

"Sounds good. See you then."

I returned to my potatoes and soon had them finished. Stewart didn't like to indulge much in conversation while he cooked, so I kept quiet while I worked. I did tell him the potatoes were done, and he stepped away from the stove.

"Thanks. I'll take over from here," he said.

I examined the pots on the stove and found green beans, purple hull peas, and carrots cooking. The oven was on, but I didn't know what was inside.

"What's in the oven?" I asked.

"Two chickens, lemon pepper and rosemary. One of each, that is," Stewart said. "I'll put some rolls in later."

"If you need me to do anything else, I will," I said.

"Not at the moment. Peeling the potatoes lightened my load enough."

"Will Haskell be here?" I asked.

"No, he's working."

I left Stewart to his meal preparations after that. I felt extraordinarily spoiled. Between Azalea during the week and Stewart on weekends, I often didn't have to do any cooking. This morning's breakfast was the exception.

"Come on, Diesel," I said. "Let Stewart do his thing, and don't beg."

The cat meowed but followed me out of the room. I had noticed him watching Stewart carefully, hoping for some kind of tidbit, but Stewart had apparently been too concentrated on his work to notice.

The doorbell rang before we reached the den. Diesel scampered off at the sound. He always wanted to be there to greet whoever was on the other side.

To my great surprise, I beheld Madame and Anton du Jardin when I opened the door.

Madame offered me a gracious smile. "You will permit the intrusion, I hope, Mr. Harris. This foolish one has done something *incroyable,* and now we must talk to someone about it. *Idiot,*" she hissed at her ex-husband.

Anton looked mutinous and started to protest, but Madame cut him off. "Quiet."

218

She turned back to me, her gracious smile once more in place. "May we come in?"

"Of course, please do." I stepped back to let them enter.

Madame had taken a couple of steps before she caught sight of Diesel. She shrieked, and at first I thought my cat had frightened her. But it was quite the opposite. I couldn't begin to translate what she was saying, but the rapturous tone of the words made it plain that she found Diesel handsome and wonderful.

Anton stood nearby and scowled at them and at me.

Diesel naturally took this adoration as his due, once he recovered from the shriek. He purred and chirped for Madame, and she ignored the cat hair clinging to her dark skirt and black tights. *"C'est merveilleux, ce chat."*

That French I understood. My cat was marvelous. "He would agree with you, Madame, most heartily. Please, won't you come into the living room?"

Diesel accompanied Madame into the living room, where she chose the sofa, apparently so Diesel could jump beside her and continue to be adored.

Anton, still scowling, slumped into a chair. "What is it I can help you with, Madame?"

I asked, hoping to get her to the point. I couldn't imagine what she wanted from me.

"We hear about you, this fool and I," Madame said. "A lady at the hotel, the one who manages the parties, she told us that you work with the police, *comme Hercule Poirot.* Is that true?"

I would have a nice chat with Donna Evans the next time I saw her and ask her not to go recommending me to anyone. I smiled at Madame to cover my irritation.

"Not precisely, Madame. Poirot was a professional who was paid for his work. I have occasionally assisted the authorities here, but I am not a professional."

Madame waved that away. "This lady says the police have respect for you, and that is good enough. She shows us the telephone book, and we find where you live. So, we are here." Her expression grew dark, and she pointed at Anton and made a spitting sound. I thought she spat on the floor, but I didn't see any evidence. "This man, he threatened to harm my poor Luc, and he must go to the police and confess. You will go with him, please."

TWENTY

I stared at Madame, not quite sure I had heard her correctly. Anton had threatened Lombardi? Threatened what?

"Can you explain for me, Madame?" I asked. "Why would Anton threaten Luke?"

Madame made the spitting sound again, and Anton glared at her. He muttered something under his breath, but I didn't understand what he said.

Madame looked contemptuous. "This one made a pass, as you say, at the handsome young man who wrote the play. He did not think Luc knew about it, but Luc threatened to fire him if he continued such behavior. Anton shouted at Luc and said he would harm him." Suddenly she threw back her head and began to wail.

"Shut up. *C'est une femme stupide.*" He, too, made that spitting sound. "I will hit you if you do not shut up."

221

Madame's wailing ceased. "You would not dare."

"Please, both of you, no more of this," I said. "I can't help you if you continue to behave this way."

"Tu es un barbare," Madame said to Anton before she turned to me. "This is why I divorce this man, you understand? I find out he likes young men, not a beautiful, mature woman like me." Her eyes flashed. "Luc adored me."

"You adore Luke's money," Anton said, looking disgusted. "I appreciated his gift."

I noticed he had not denied her revelations of his sexuality.

"Excuse me, Anton, but did you argue with your employer over the playwright?"

"We did," Anton replied.

"Was it the first one, the one with the red hair, or the second one, who turned out to be the real playwright?" I asked.

"The second one," Anton said. "The first one looked like *un pitre.*"

I thought that meant *clown,* and I asked Anton.

He nodded. "He was also like a giraffe, much too tall," he added.

This was all rather bizarre, I decided. I really didn't understand what they expected me to do.

"Madame, I need to understand this more." I offered her an apologetic smile. "Lombardi and Anton had a fight over the young playwright. Does this mean Lombardi was interested in him as well? I mean, in the same way Anton was?"

Madame laughed. "Oh, I assure you, no, he was not. It is this way, you see. Whenever Anton falls in love, he becomes obsessed. It is always the grand passion with him. He walks around like a girl who worships a movie star. You understand?"

I cast a quick glance at Anton, who was still glowering at Madame, and I couldn't say that I blamed him.

"You mean he neglects his duties at these times?" I asked.

She gave an emphatic nod. "Yes, that is it. My Luc could not tolerate this behavior. His wardrobe, it must be perfect. You understand? This one forgets how to press the clothes when he is lovestruck."

"Apparently this kind of thing has happened before?" I asked. When Madame nodded, I hurried on before she could elaborate. "Then why was this time so different? Why would Anton threaten Lombardi?"

Madame shrugged. "I do not know. Usually this one pouts and gets on with his work. This time, who knows? Perhaps Luc thinks the young man will be interested and lure him away." From her tone it was obvious to me that she found the idea ridiculous.

"Was this the case?" I asked Anton.

He shrugged. "He liked me," he said simply.

I took a moment to consider how to handle this. I could imagine Kanesha listening to this, and I had to suppress a smile.

"I'm not sure this would make the police believe that Anton really wanted to kill Lombardi," I said, and Madame started to bridle. "But they do need to know about it. They need every piece of information so they can find the truth. I will be happy to call the detective in charge of the investigation. I know she will want to talk to you."

Madame regarded me with a smile. "That is good. Yes, that is what we want."

I wondered why Anton was going along with this so docilely. Was he so intimidated by his former wife that he did whatever she told him to? Something about this didn't ring true, but I couldn't figure out what that was. The whole situation seemed like a farce from a French play.

"All right, then." I pulled out my cell phone and called Kanesha's personal number. To my surprise she answered right away.

I explained the situation, and she asked me to bring them to the sheriff's department. I agreed to, though it wasn't at all convenient.

I put my phone away. "Chief Deputy Berry is ready to talk to you," I said. "She would like you to come to her office, however."

Madame immediately pushed herself up from the couch, and she snapped her fingers at Anton. "Come, we must go."

"I'll be happy to drive you," I said.

"But no, we have a taxi. He waits for us," Madame said. "You have done enough for us. Come, Anton, we must go to this office of the sheriff lady."

I escorted them to the front door, and I did see a taxi waiting in front of my house. I bade them goodbye and shut the door on Madame hectoring Anton all the way down the walk to the street.

I should have realized they hadn't walked here from the Farrington House, but their appearance on my doorstep had evidently scrambled my thinking processes. I headed for the kitchen with Diesel.

"Who was at the door?" Stewart asked.

I told him about Madame and Anton and what they wanted, and Stewart started laughing. After a moment, I joined him. Now that they were gone, I really could see

225

the ridiculous side of the whole incident.

When he finally stopped laughing, he said, "These two are like characters in some French farce. I wonder whether they're really like this, or are they putting on an act, and if so, why?"

"Same here," I said. "I wonder if they really are going to the sheriff's department to talk to Kanesha."

"If they don't show up there soon, I bet Kanesha will call you," Stewart said.

I grimaced. "I'm sure you're right."

"Do you think what they told you is the truth?" Stewart asked before he turned back to the stove.

"It's possible, I suppose. Maybe a version of the truth," I said.

"What do you mean by that?"

"That Anton did argue with Lombardi and threaten him, but not over his making a pass at Ulrich Dingelbach," I said.

"All Kanesha has to do is ask Dingelbach if Anton made a pass at him," Stewart pointed out. "If he didn't, bang goes their story."

"True, but I wouldn't be surprised if Anton did make the pass, at some point *after* he'd argued with Lombardi, and that the two aren't connected."

"That's possible, I suppose," Stewart said.

"But what other reason might Anton have to threaten Lombardi?"

"Lombardi didn't treat him very well," I said, "and maybe the worm finally turned. There is something so obsequious about Anton, I think."

"What a lovely thought." Stewart laughed. "So, basically you think they've come up with this story to mask the real motive for the fight, hoping the police won't find it out and will dismiss this story for being too ridiculous."

"Yes," I said. "And not give the matter any further thought."

"But they don't know Kanesha, do they?"

"No, they don't, and they could find themselves in a tight spot if they aren't careful," I said. "Kanesha has no patience for time wasters."

"What if they're telling the truth?" Stewart asked. "What do you think? Did Anton kill Lombardi?"

"No, not for the reason they gave me. Yes, I know the stereotype of the passionate Frenchman and the so-called crime of passion. That kind of crime happens, but in this case, I don't think it did. I think they're trying to hide something, but Kanesha will have to sort it out."

"You don't want to have to deal with

them, do you?" Stewart sounded sympathetic.

"No, I don't," I said. "They confuse me. I have no idea what to think, whether they're telling anything remotely like the truth or making up something ridiculous just to confuse the issue."

"There is one point to keep in mind," Stewart said.

"What's that?"

"No one else here knew Lombardi, other than Laura, and we both know she didn't play those pranks or kill him. Why would some stranger here in Athena want him dead?"

I hadn't considered the situation from this angle, and I had to admit that Stewart had an excellent point.

"So you think it's more likely that Madame or Anton is the killer since they were the only ones who knew him well?"

"Maybe they did it together," Stewart said.

"Possibly," I said. "But actually, Laura isn't the only person in Athena who knew Lombardi."

"Who would the other person be?"

"Persons," I said. "Melba and a friend of hers saw him in a play in New York a few years ago. One of the supporting actors in the cast was the friend's nephew. The friend was Katrinka Krause. Do you know her?"

"Reddish hair, high cheekbones, and an arresting face?" Stewart asked.

"Yes, that's her," I said.

"I don't know her personally, but a few years ago, she dated one of the assistant professors in my department," he said. "They broke up after about six months, I think, but she stuck in my mind. I see her every once in a while on campus." He went to the sink to wash his hands. "So, we know Melba didn't kill this guy. Do you think Katrinka Krause could have?"

"It's possible," I said. "Or her nephew."

"What are their motives?" Stewart poured himself some tea and joined me at the table.

I related Melba's story, about the encounter in New York and the subsequent firing of Katrinka's nephew.

"Possibly a motive," Stewart said. "But that seems pretty extreme just for losing a job, even one on Broadway."

"I agree with you, but there's another part of the story. Katrinka showed up at the reception for Lombardi last Saturday, and I can tell you, she wasn't trying to get away from him. She was actively coming on to him." I told Stewart about the ensuing scene with Madame.

"Strange that her attitude would change

229

so dramatically, but maybe she planned to seduce him, get him somewhere, and humiliate him in revenge for what Lombardi did to her nephew. That seems more likely to me than her actually murdering the guy."

"Can't argue with you," I said. "That's the thing that's frustrating me, and I imagine it's going to frustrate Kanesha, too. Why did somebody want Luke Lombardi dead?"

Neither of us could answer that, and I suspected that the real motive was going to be hard to figure out without some big break in the case. Kanesha's bailiwick, not mine, though I wasn't going to stop keeping an eye on things for Laura's sake. I had believed Kanesha when she said she didn't really think Laura was a killer. That didn't mean I wouldn't be ready to throw myself in the ring, so to speak, if necessary.

Stewart and I had exhausted the possibilities with Madame and Anton, so we talked about the first act of the play.

"I thought Laura was terrific," Stewart said. "The energy between her and Lombardi was amazing. I don't know how they did it, but it was captivating. I couldn't take my eyes off them."

I was pleased that he'd had the same reaction I'd had. "Yes, I thought so, too. I was so proud of her, and I think the play would have been a huge triumph for all concerned, had it not been for Lombardi's death." Unbidden, the images of the actor's last moments rolled in my brain, and I shuddered.

"It was truly one of the most horrible things I've ever seen," Stewart said.

"Yes, it was."

The kitchen door to the garage opened, and Helen Louise came in, a large covered cake plate held expertly in one hand. I got up to take it from her and set it on the table; then I turned to give her a hug and a kiss.

"Hello, stranger," I said when I released her.

She laughed. "I know. It seems forever, doesn't it? But it was only a week ago that I was here." She dumped her bag on the table and pulled out a chair. Diesel immediately demanded her attention, and she supplied it. "So what's new?" she asked.

Stewart and I shared a glance. Now the time had come. I had to confess to Helen Louise that I was involved in another murder case.

TWENTY-ONE

When neither Stewart nor I responded right away to her question, Helen Louise frowned. "What gives? Surely the question isn't that hard to understand."

Stewart snorted with laughter.

I threw him a cease-and-desist look before I answered Helen Louise. "You haven't heard about what happened during the play last night, obviously." I hoped against hope that she had somehow found out since we talked earlier.

Helen Louise's expression froze. Then she shook her head. "Come on, Charlie, you're not going to tell me somebody got murdered during the play? Or maybe in the audience?"

I sighed heavily. "Yes, Luke Lombardi was murdered at the beginning of the second act."

"Incroyable," Helen Louise said, her mingled disgust and awe apparent in those few

syllables.

"Yes, it is unbelievable," I said, "but my presence had nothing to do with it."

"I should hope not," Helen Louise said. "Was Laura onstage at the time?"

"Yes, she was, and she was supposed to drink from the same bottle that killed Lombardi," I said.

Helen Louise paled. "Oh, merciful heaven, she didn't. Please tell me she didn't."

"No, she didn't. Sorry. I should have said that immediately," I told her contritely.

"As long as Laura is okay," Helen Louise said, "I forgive you."

Stewart got out the wine and poured a glass for Helen Louise. "Here." He handed her the glass. "I think you need this."

"I think I do," Helen Louise said. "I've been thinking of nothing but work, work, work, all week. I'll be delirious with joy when Henry is back, which should be sometime this afternoon."

"I haven't told you about any of the incidents that occurred earlier this week," I said. "I knew you were working really hard and needed to focus on the bistro. I didn't want you to be worrying about anything else."

"Thank you, love. I appreciate the consideration," Helen Louise said after a couple of sips of wine. "But now I want to hear it all. Do we have time before everyone arrives?"

"Maybe," I said.

"Talk, and I promise not to interrupt," she said.

I managed to tell her everything except about the interview earlier this morning with Madame and Anton. Laura and Frank arrived with baby Charlie, and I changed the subject the minute I heard the adults' voices at the front door.

"I'll tell you the rest later," I said.

Alex and Sean, with Rosie in her carrier, arrived shortly after the others. Helen Louise assisted Stewart with transferring the food to the table in the dining room. Stewart must have set the table before he started cooking, and I felt guilty that I hadn't even thought about getting the table ready for the meal.

I sat at the head of the table and Helen Louise at the foot. The others took their usual places along the sides, and the babies were in a playpen in a corner of the room. Diesel, the self-appointed baby watcher, was on duty, ready to alert us the moment either Rosie or Charlie needed something.

I asked Sean to say grace today, and he did so beautifully. When he finished, we began helping ourselves and sending the food around the table until everyone was served.

I hadn't had a chance to get Laura to myself. She looked good, I thought, given the trauma of the night before. The slight shadows under her eyes let me know that she hadn't slept quite as well as Frank had led me to believe. I knew my daughter's sensitive, vulnerable heart, and she would grieve for Luke Lombardi, despite their differences. No matter what he had done, he hadn't deserved such a merciless death.

Stewart was the first to introduce the subject of the play and its abrupt conclusion. "You might not want to hear this now, Laura and Frank, but I have to tell you, that first act was superb. I congratulate you on the production and Laura's amazing performance."

Laura looked like she was going to cry, and Frank merely looked uncomfortable.

"Stewart is right, Sis," Sean said. "What happened in the second act was horrendous, and I know you can't help thinking about it. But you should be proud of yourself. I could hardly believe that woman onstage was my baby sister, the one who used to act out the plots of Nancy Drew books with her dolls." He grinned at her.

"Thank you," she said. "It *is* hard to think about the good part, because I feel so guilty about the horrible part. I won't ever forget poor Luke, lying there like that." She grabbed her glass and gulped down some iced tea.

"That wasn't your fault," I said. "I know it's hard, but you have to remember that. Luke's death was the act of a cold, ruthless person, and it was not you. It could never be you."

Everyone else spoke up then, echoing my comments, and Laura smiled her thanks. "Can we talk about something else for a bit?" she asked.

Stewart shot me an impish glance. "Charlie, why don't you tell everyone about the visit from Madame and Anton this morning? That ought to give everyone a few chuckles."

The interview had had its comic moments, I realized, and I played those up as I related the story. Helen Louise, Sean, and Frank laughed in the appropriate places, while Alex and Laura shook their heads in disbelief. When I finished, the first comment came from Helen Louise.

"Like something out of Molière," she said. "I wonder what they're hoping to get out of such an idiotic story."

"It's not completely idiotic," Laura said. "I did hear Anton and Luke screaming at each other one day." She paused and frowned. "The question is, which day was it?"

"Was it before Ulrich Dingelbach turned up?" I asked.

"No, I don't think so," Laura said. "Maybe it was that same evening, after we finished the run-through. I was in my dressing room, and the walls aren't that thick, you know, so I could hear Anton and Luke carrying on in the next room."

"What were they talking about?" Sean asked.

"I couldn't make it out. They were arguing in French." She flashed at look at Helen Louise. "I needed you there to interpret for me."

"I wish I had been there," Helen Louise replied. "This fascinates me. Tell me, had you had any idea before now that Anton was gay?"

"No," Laura said. "I'd have said he was asexual, if anything, based on my experience of him when Luke and I worked together before. But it could explain why Madame divorced him. That and the fact that he never had much money. Luke made a lot, I think, given his work record, and he was careful with it. I don't think Anton could afford to quit. Madame has expensive tastes."

"So Madame dumped her husband and went straight for the source of the cash?" Alex said. "How mercenary."

"In my experience," Helen Louise said, "some women always keep their eye on the money, and I believe Madame is such a woman. She is not sentimental as far as I can tell."

"If Anton and Luke weren't arguing about Anton's making a pass at Dingelbach," Frank said, "then what *were* they arguing about?"

"That is precisely what Kanesha is going to have to find out," I said. "More power to her if she can get it out of those two. I'm not sure I have the patience to deal with them again."

"I hope you won't have anything more to do with them, Dad," Sean said. "Whoever killed Lombardi is cold-blooded. You don't want to draw his attention to you."

A chill crept over the room with those words. No one spoke for a moment; then I broke the silence. "I'm aware of that, Sean, and I do not intend to do anything to draw the killer's attention, I promise you. Now, let's talk about something else." I looked at

Stewart. Trouper that he was, he came through.

Stewart began to describe a really awful movie he and Haskell had watched recently. Stewart was an excellent raconteur, and he soon had everyone's spirits lifted.

"Why on earth did you keep watching this movie if it was that bad?" Alex demanded. "I'd have turned it off after about ten minutes, if not sooner."

"Ah, my dear Alex," Stewart said, "you have obviously not discovered the joy of watching something awful simply because it *is* awful. The best part of this movie was the fact that the actors and the director were utterly serious. They thought the script was good, their performances were good, and so on, but it was all too, too dreadful."

"Sounds rather sad to me," Alex said.

"They had absolutely no sense of humor. Anyone who could utter such inane lines as 'The peace of the world is our burden and our blessing, Alice. We are the progenitors of all that is, and will be, good. Mankind will look back upon us as saviors,' was obviously taking himself entirely too seriously."

Alex laughed. "I see your point. That's dreadful."

"I've seen that movie!" Sean exclaimed. "We watched it once in the dorm at college.

I remember we howled over it, too."

The conversation moved on from there, and I was happy to enjoy my food and listen to the others talk. From time to time, Helen Louise and I exchanged smiles. These family dinners were the high point of every week. I hoped the tradition continued for many years to come.

After we collectively consumed Helen Louise's delicious chocolate cake, along with scoops of vanilla ice cream, we cleared the table. I finally got a chance to talk to Laura for a moment alone when everyone else had left the kitchen.

"How are you doing?" I asked, slipping an arm around her and hugging her tight.

"I'm doing okay, Dad." She rested her head against my shoulder. "Last night the most horrifying thing imaginable happened. I detested Luke, honestly, but I'd never want him to die like that."

"I know, sweetheart," I said. "I'm so thankful that you didn't drink your tea."

"I still don't know why I didn't," Laura said. "I've gone over it and over it, and I simply don't understand why I waited."

"Don't question a miracle," I said. "I'm not going to."

"Please be careful," Laura said. "The man who did this is completely heartless."

"I know, and I'm not anxious to grab his attention," I said. "You tell your brother I intend to keep my nose as clean as possible, okay?" *Unless one of my loved ones is in danger, and I can do something to make them safe.*

Laura smiled wanly up at me. "I will, Dad. Sean will be happy to hear it. We kinda like having you around, you know. No more shenanigans like last time."

"I like being around." I pushed her away. "Isn't it about time you fed my grandson?"

"Yes, it is, as a matter of fact. I'd better do it before he starts yelling his head off. He's like his grandfather. When he wants his food, he gets grumpy." She hurried out of the kitchen before I could come up with a suitable retort.

Helen Louise came in a moment later. "How are you doing, love? You didn't say much today after you told your story."

"I'm fine," I said, pulling her close. "I was happy to listen."

She kissed my cheek. "The patriarch benignly surveys his family."

"I suppose," I said. "Listen, I want to ask you about Madame and Anton. You've had a lot of experience with the French. Are they typical, would you say?"

"I certainly encountered a few women of

Madame's ilk in Paris," Helen Louise said. "Anton is your garden-variety loser, I'd say. You can find their types in every nationality. We've both known people like them right here in Athena."

"Yes, you're right," I said.

Helen Louise continued. "Their story sounds far-fetched to me, but I've seen and heard wilder things, both here and in France."

"I can't help thinking it's all a smoke screen," I said, "but there are other suspects." I reminded her about Jared Eckworth, and Katrinka Krause and her nephew.

"The only motive that sounds strong enough, and it's not that strong, is the young actor's," Helen Louise said. "I've dealt with ambitious men before, and I knew at least two who would have knifed someone in the back without thinking twice about it, if it meant they got what they wanted."

"That scares me," I said. "I hope neither of those men is anywhere around here."

"No, they're not," Helen Louise said. "Let's join the others in the living room."

"Good idea." I followed her out of the kitchen.

During the next hour, no one brought up

the subject of plays, death, or murder, and we talked of family things and plans for the summer. By the time my children gathered up their children and departed, Stewart, Helen Louise, and I all were ready for a glass of wine and a quieter house.

"Have you talked to Melba since last night?" Helen Louise asked.

"No, I haven't," I said. "The last I saw of her was when I left her and the Ducotes to go onstage to Laura."

"Why don't you check on her?" Stewart said. "I never got a chance to talk to her last night at all. To the sisters, either."

I pulled out my phone and called Melba. She answered right away, as if she had been waiting for the call.

"How are you doing?" I asked. "I'm sitting here with Helen Louise and Stewart, and we thought we ought to check on you."

"I'm doing good. Wasn't last night horrible?" Melba said. "Miss An'gel invited me to go with them after we were allowed to leave to have a drink in the bar at the Farrington House, and I took her up on it."

"That was nice of her," I said.

"It sure was," Melba said, "and you'll never guess who I saw there."

"No, I'm sure I won't, so you go ahead and tell me," I said.

"Katrinka's nephew, Micah," she said. "I had no idea he was in town."

TWENTY-TWO

"Are you sure about this?" I asked Melba. Helen Louise and Stewart caught my sharp tone and leaned closer. "I'm going to put you on speakerphone."

"Okay," Melba said.

I put the phone on the table so that the others could hear.

"Ready?" Melba asked.

"Yes," we three said in unison.

Diesel perked up when he heard Melba's voice, and he looked around to find her. As she continued to talk, the cat paced around the room, obviously puzzled because he couldn't see her. I tried to get him to sit by me, but he kept looking.

"All right, then," Melba replied. "Yes, I'm sure. I've seen the boy a couple of times, although the last time was when we were in New York to see that play he was in."

"Are you by yourself?" I asked, suddenly remembering Katrinka Krause.

"Yes. Why?" Melba asked.

"Because what I have to talk to you about isn't for anyone else's ears, specifically not your friend Katrinka's," I explained.

"What does Katrinka have to do with this? Or Micah?"

"I'm about to explain that to you," I said. "I remembered the story you told me about what happened backstage when you and Katrinka went back to see Micah, and Luke Lombardi started hitting on Katrinka."

"Yes, and she didn't like it, but that creep wouldn't leave her alone. Micah got involved, and it ended up costing his job," Melba said. "So?"

"So Katrinka was at the reception at the Farrington House last Saturday evening. She met Lombardi again, and this time she was the one hitting on Lombardi."

"You must be mistaken," Melba said. "How do you know it was Katrinka? You said you didn't know her."

"I didn't," I said, "until I met her that day at your house, when I brought you the quiche you wanted. Remember?"

"Oh, yeah, I forgot about that. So you had already seen this woman at the party, and you're sure it was Katrinka?"

"Yes, I'm sure. Your friend is a striking woman. Stewart knows her, too. Once you've seen her, you're not going to forget her."

"Yeah, I guess you're right." Melba sounded a little sour. "I don't understand why she'd be at the party making goo-goo eyes at that actor."

"I don't, either, unless she had an ulterior motive," I said.

"Now, what kind of motive . . ." She trailed off, after starting out sounding pretty annoyed with me. "I get where you're going with this. If you think Katrinka killed that guy, you're crazy, Charlie Harris. She's not that kind of woman. I can tell you that."

"Why is her nephew in town? Do you know?"

The abrupt switch of subjects threw Melba off a bit.

"What's Micah got to do with it?"

I waited for her to catch up.

"Now look here, Charlie. Micah is a nice young man. He came down from New York to visit family, mainly his aunt, because she's about all he has left, except a few cousins hereabouts. You think he'd kill that man because he got fired from a play? That's nuts."

Before I could say anything, Melba continued. "Stewart, I know you're listening. Helen Louise, you, too. Is Charlie drunk?

247

What have y'all been giving him to drink? He's losing it, big-time."

Stewart laughed, and Helen Louise bit back a smile. Stewart said, "Now, Melba, you know Charlie better than that. He's had only one glass of wine today."

"Yes, Melba," Helen Louise said. "I can vouch for him. He's completely sober."

"I understand your feelings about your friend and her nephew," I said, mustering the few shreds of patience I could, "but someone killed that man and came near to killing my daughter, too. I'm not messing around on this, Melba. I want whoever did this behind bars as quick as possible."

"What do you mean, came near to killing Laura?" Melba sounded upset.

I quickly explained.

"Oh, Charlie, honey, I'm so sorry. No wonder you're so worried about this. I understand where you're coming from now." She sighed. "Thank the Lord Laura wasn't hurt."

"Thank you," I said. "I appreciate that."

"You know I love that daughter of yours," Melba said gently. "Even so, I still don't think Katrinka or Micah was involved. I understand, though, that they need to talk to the cops. And Katrinka needs to explain to me what she thought she was doing, playing the hussy to that creep."

Stewart rolled his eyes at that, and Helen Louise grinned. Melba was going to be Melba, no matter what.

"You said you saw Micah. Where was that?" I asked, momentarily blank.

"At the Farrington House after the play last night. I caught a glimpse of him and Katrinka. That was the first I knew he was in town," Melba replied.

Helen Louise, Stewart, and I looked at one another. This could be significant.

"Do you have any idea how long he's been in town?" Stewart asked.

"No, I don't. Katrinka didn't mention anything about it to me," Melba said. "He may have flown down yesterday for all I know, or he could have been here several days. Is it important when he got here?"

"It could be," I said. "If he didn't arrive until today, then he is definitely not involved in this case, except perhaps tangentially."

"Because of Katrinka, you mean," Melba said flatly.

"Yes." I couldn't sugarcoat this. "If he has been here for several days, he could be the one who was playing the pranks on Lombardi. Including the one that killed him."

"What pranks? What are you talking about?" Melba asked.

I gave her a quick rundown on the tricks played on Lombardi, leading up to his death onstage.

Melba sighed. "I can't see Micah doing any of that, especially not poisoning that actor. He's not a vindictive young man. But I'll call Katrinka and ask her about it. I was figuring on talking to her anyway about last night. I'll let you know what I find out. Talk to you later."

We all said goodbye to her, and I ended the call.

"Melba is loyal to her friends," Helen Louise said. "You can't fault her for that."

"I don't," I said. "She has been the greatest of friends to me since I moved back to Athena. If Katrinka or Micah is involved in this, I'm sorry, but whoever killed Lombardi has to be found and put away."

Now that he no longer heard his friend's voice, Diesel stopped wandering around the room and came to stretch out on the floor by my chair. I wished I could explain to him why he couldn't see Melba, and I might have tried if Stewart and Helen Louise hadn't been in the room. Diesel might have understood me. I simply never knew with him. He was such a smart cat.

"No one is arguing that point," Stewart said. "We all want that. But I have to say, I think the potential motives that Katrinka and her nephew have are not that strong."

"Okay, then, who has the strongest motive?" I asked, slightly nettled. I wasn't really annoyed with Stewart, I realized. The sense of urgency I felt over this stemmed from fear. I didn't want the killer to have the chance to harm anyone else, especially not my Laura.

"There isn't much to choose from, is there?" Stewart said. "I think the young actor bears looking at a little more deeply. I can't help but think about the movie *All About Eve* in this situation. Eve didn't resort to murder in the movie, but she might have. That kind of ruthless ambition doesn't go around impediments — it destroys them."

I had seen the movie to which Stewart referred, a couple of times, and I understood the reference. In the movie, the stakes were much bigger, because the story centered on Broadway.

"Point taken," I said, "but this isn't Broadway. It's a small-town college production."

Stewart nodded. "Yes, but Eve had to start somewhere. She didn't just pop up in full bloom on Broadway."

"That's an excellent point," Helen Louise said. "Eve left her footprints on the backs of quite a few people, I'm sure, before she did it to Margo Channing." She sighed. "I do love Bette Davis. I don't see how she kept from taking a knife to Anne Baxter in that movie."

After talking to Frank, I had not considered Jared Eckworth as seriously as I had before, though I hadn't given up on him as a suspect. Now, however, with Stewart and Helen Louise's opinions backing up my own feelings, I began to think I might have been right in the first place.

"Frank doesn't believe Eckworth is like that," I said. "I need to talk to Laura about him. Frank says he's in one of her classes, and she knows him a little better."

"Kanesha knows about him, doesn't she?" Helen Louise asked.

I nodded. "I told her everything."

"Good. Then she will take care of it," Stewart said. "I'm sure she'll talk to Laura about this kid."

"In other words, stay out of it," I said in a resigned tone.

Helen Louise reached over and took my right hand in both of hers. "Love, we simply want to keep you safe. Remember what happened not so long ago when you confronted a killer."

"I know." I remembered all too well. I had gotten too big for my britches, as my mother would have said, and I could have been badly hurt. "I won't make that mistake again."

Helen Louise squeezed my hand and released it. "Good."

Stewart nodded at me. "I want to be able to visit you in the nursing home, so you have to stick around. I promise I'll bring you good food so you won't have to live on the terrible food those places feed you."

That made me laugh, and I no longer felt quite so tense. Stewart grinned, and Helen Louise rolled her eyes at both of us.

Stewart pushed back his chair and stood. "As fascinating as this is, I need to get Dante and take him for a walk before he gets into my shoes again." He gave Helen Louise a quick kiss on the cheek. "See you later."

I appreciated his discretion. He wanted to give Helen Louise and me time alone together. I was about to suggest to Helen Louise that we retire to the den, where we could snuggle on the couch, but she forestalled me.

"I'm sorry, Charlie, but I have to go, too." I heard the note of regret in her voice. "Henry's due back in town in about an hour, and I promised to meet him at the bistro at five to go over the supplies so he can place orders tomorrow. I haven't been able to keep up with everything while he's been gone."

"I understand," I said. "I'm glad you found him. He's taken on a lot of responsibility, and I think he's worth every penny you pay him."

She gave me a wry smile. "I pay him a lot of pennies because I don't want him going anywhere." She hesitated. "I haven't mentioned this to you before, but Henry told me that, if I ever want to retire, he wants to buy the business. I think that's one of the reasons he decided to stay here."

"He's ambitious, too." I smiled. "What do you think of the idea?"

"He's the only person I *would* sell to," Helen Louise said. "I'm not ready to retire, however, so don't get your hopes up too soon."

"I won't," I said. "I have to point out, though, that Henry won't wait forever. He's what, maybe thirty-two or thirty-three?"

Helen Louise nodded. "He turned thirty-three this past week."

"He's not going to want to wait until he's in his forties to run his own business," I said. "He's a capable young man, and you've sung his praises to me pretty often the last six months or so."

"So I need to keep that in mind." Helen Louise sighed. "You're right, and I promise you I will be thinking about that." She suddenly rose and came to wrap her arms around me. She laid her head on top of mine. "I love you so much, not only because you're the sweetest man alive, but because you understand how much all this means to me." She released me, and I got up to pull her into my arms.

After a while, we pulled apart. Helen Louise smiled and touched my cheek. "I'll call you later on."

I nodded and watched her depart through the kitchen door. I found Diesel sitting at my feet. When he saw that I was looking at him, he placed a paw on my knee and warbled. I scratched his head.

"Yes, we're lucky, aren't we, that she loves us both so much?"

Diesel gave an enthusiastic meow.

"Come on, boy, let's go to the den and watch TV."

I got comfortable in my recliner, and Diesel stretched out on the sofa. With the TV on, set to my favorite nostalgia channel, I soon found my eyelids drooping, and I drifted into sleep.

I awoke sometime later to the ringing of my telephone. I didn't get many calls these days on the landline phone, so it took a moment for the sound to register. There was an extension on my desk here in the den, and I got up to answer it.

"Hello, Charlie Harris speaking."

"Good afternoon, Mr. Harris, I beg your pardon for disturbing you like this, but these people insisted that I call you." In the background I heard others talking, and I began to get an inkling of the situation.

"Excuse me," I said, "but who are you, if you don't mind my asking?"

"Sorry," the man said. "I'm calling from the Farrington House. I'm one of the assistant managers, Cody Cade, and we are trying to sort out a situation. But these people insist that they simply must talk to you, so I called. I didn't know what else to do."

"All right, Mr. Cade," I said. "Are the people in question Madame du Jardin and Anton du Jardin?"

"Yes. How did you know?" the assistant managed sounded surprised.

"I can hear them in the background."

There was a brief pause, and I heard garbled voices. Then Madame spoke into the receiver.

"You must come at once. These people here will not listen to me. They insist we must leave because we cannot pay, and I tell them no, we will not go. You must come and explain to them." The receiver crashed down on the other end.

Twenty-Three

How had I become the zookeeper? I wondered. I did not want to have to deal with Madame and Anton anymore today. I was tempted simply to call Frank and tell him he had to handle it. They were no responsibility of mine, after all.

After dithering for a couple of minutes, I did call Frank and tell him what was going on. He groaned.

"I'm heading down there in a minute," I said. "I'll try to get everyone calmed down. Is there anything you can do about the hotel bill?"

"I'll see what I can do," Frank said. "They were all supposed to check out today and be driven back to the airport in Memphis. Our budget can stand only so much, but I guess, given the circumstances, we'll have to cover their bills. Let me make a couple of calls, and I'll see what I can do."

"Thanks," I said. "I hated to bother you,

but I thought you needed to know about it."

"It's okay, Charlie," Frank said. "One of the joys of being a department head. I'll call your cell phone when I get things sorted out." He ended the call.

"Diesel, would you like to come with me?" I looked over at the cat, still resting on the sofa. He perked up right away and slid off the sofa. I figured taking him with me might help to defuse the situation, since Madame had made such a fuss over him this morning.

When we reached the Farrington House, the lobby was relatively quiet. No outbursts in French, no histrionics from Madame. I found her and Anton seated in the area off the lobby filled with comfortable chairs and a couple of sofas. Madame saw me and Diesel, and she smiled. Anton scowled. I decided that was his only expression.

"You are so kind." Madame beamed at me. "And you have brought the so beautiful *chat* with you. Come, my darling, sit by your *tante Delphine.*"

Diesel needed no further urging. He hopped onto the sofa beside Madame and allowed her to stroke him and whisper to him in French. Anton looked at the two and sniffed. I took a chair facing Anton and sideways to Madame and Diesel.

"I will do what I can to help," I said. "What exactly is the problem here?"

To my surprise, Anton replied, "They say we should have *checked out* earlier today because the rooms were reserved only through last night. We try to explain to them the problem. The lady sheriff insists we must stay in this town until she knows who slaughtered my poor master." He shrugged. "We have nowhere else to go. We have no money."

"This is true," Madame said. "My Luc, he held the purse strings. Is that how you say it?" After I nodded, she continued. "Anton and me, we have almost no money of our own, you understand."

"I see the problem," I replied. "I have talked to my son-in-law, Frank, and he is going to see what he can do about the situation. Let me go talk to the manager, and I will be back shortly. Do you mind if Diesel stays with you?"

"Not at all. You are so kind." Madame beamed at me again.

I left them there and approached the desk. I found a harassed-looking young man of about thirty standing there, fiddling with various things on the desk. He didn't look familiar to me.

"Are you Mr. Cade?" I asked. He nodded. "I'm Charlie Harris."

He immediately looked relieved. "Thank you so much for coming, Mr. Harris. I hope you can make these people understand the situation. They were supposed to check out this morning, but they were nowhere around when we went to their rooms to inquire, and then they suddenly turned up about two hours ago. We don't know what to do with them."

I listened to the rapid spate of words until he ran out of breath. Then, before he could get going again, I said, "I do understand the situation from your point of view. But there is a complicating factor in all this. Mr. Lombardi died onstage last night during the performance of the play. He was their employer" — I didn't want to get into Madame's relationship with the late actor — "and they have little money. They can't pay."

I held up a hand as the manager drew breath to talk. "They have been here as guests of the theater department at the college. My son-in-law, Frank Salisbury, is the head of the department. He is working on this situation, and I should be hearing from him soon. In the meantime, are their rooms available for tonight, and perhaps longer?"

"I'll check," the manager said.

I waited for him to play with his computer, and after about two minutes, he looked up at me. "We have the space, and they can stay in their rooms for the next five days, but after that, we're booked solid." He frowned. "We have to have assurance that their bills will be paid, however."

"Frank will take care of that," I said. "I'll call him and let him know they can keep the rooms for now. I'll have him call you to confirm the particulars. How's that?"

"Thank you so much, Mr. Harris," Cody said. "I hated to bother you, but they wouldn't stop insisting that I call you. Thank goodness you're listed in the phone book, or I don't know what I would have done."

"It's okay. I'm happy to help." I smiled at him and turned away from the desk. I wasn't keen on returning to Madame and Anton, but I had agreed to do this.

I debated going to the bar first but decided against it. I walked back to where Madame and Anton sat glaring at each other. Diesel didn't look happy, and I knew he felt uncomfortable because of the tension between the couple. I resumed my seat and called to the cat. "Here, Diesel."

He pulled away from Madame and

stretched out on the carpet beside me. Madame appeared peeved by his defection but did not protest.

"You have made all well again?" she asked.

"Partially," I said. "You can keep your rooms for a few more days, but the hotel insists that someone guarantees payment. I'm hoping Frank can arrange that."

"Such a handsome young man, that Frank," Madame practically cooed. She pronounced the name in the French manner, with the broad *ah* sound. "So strong, so forceful, he even made my Luc pay attention."

Anton grunted.

"Bah." She spat at her ex-husband. "This one here, he likes them small and not so masculine as Frank."

I wanted to comment that Frank would have been relieved to hear it, but that sounded more like something Stewart might have said. And probably would have, had he been here, I reflected.

"You talked to Chief Deputy Berry," I said. "How did that go?"

"She is very smart, that one," Madame said. "She will find out who murdered my Luc." Her lower lip quivered for a moment, and I was afraid she would burst into tears. She managed to control herself, however. "I tell her everything I know, *naturellement.* She respects another woman — I can always tell — and understands I tell her the truth."

I wished I dared ask Kanesha what she thought of Madame and her honesty. I wondered if Kanesha's opinion differed on this subject.

I glanced at Anton. "What about you? Did you tell her everything as well?"

Anton rolled his eyes. "When I could speak, I did." He flung out a hand toward Madame. "With that one who talks like a volcano erupting, it is hard to be heard. You understand?"

Madame glared at each of us in turn, and I could see no polite way out of this situation.

"It's a difficult time for both of you," I said, "and emotions are running high. I'm sure it's painful for you both to talk about your loss."

Madame appeared satisfied, but Anton returned to his habitual scowl.

Despite their current emotional states, I didn't hesitate to ask them a question I had been wanting to put to them.

"Do you know if Mr. Lombardi left a will? Did he have a lawyer?"

Anton, to my surprise, answered, "He has *un avocat* in Los Angeles." He patted the pocket in his shirt. "In my little book I have his name and phone number. I give it to the sheriff lady already."

"That's good. I know she appreciated your help."

He hadn't answered my question about a will, and I was about to ask again when Madame spoke.

"There is a will," she said. "My Luc, he showed it to me. I get everything. I was the love of his life, you understand." Her expression turned tragic.

Anton growled. "You did not tell me this, Delphine. There is nothing for me, after I work so hard for him? *Connard.*" He shouted the last word.

Madame's expression was now one of pity. "No, he did not leave you anything except his clothes. You can sell those, can you not?"

"Pah, what are they worth to me? I have nothing else but his clothes?" His voice rose steadily, and he switched to French. He sounded furious, and I couldn't say I blamed him.

The young manager joined us. "You must be quiet, sir. You're disturbing the other guests. You'll have to leave if you continue this disruption."

Anton stopped and glared at the manager, but he subsided, looking sulky. The manager flounced off, his smile triumphant.

I prayed that Frank would call soon so I could go back home. Diesel had tried to get under my chair while Anton was ranting, but he managed only to get his head there. I stroked his back.

My phone rang then, and I'd never been so glad to hear it.

"Yes, Frank," I said.

"You sound frazzled," he replied.

"Yes, that's the situation," I said.

Frank coughed. "You're off the hook, Charlie. I managed to get the college to agree to pay their expenses through Friday. By then, hopefully, this thing will be resolved, and they can go away."

"That is terrific news. Thanks."

"I hope you have a bottle of wine ready at home," Frank said. "By now you need it, I'm sure."

"Like you wouldn't believe," I said. "I'll give them the news."

"I'm calling the hotel next, but I wanted to let you know first." He ended the call.

I faced Madame feeling much better, knowing that I would be free of these people once I gave them the news. "That was Frank," I said. "He has arranged for the college to pay your expenses until Friday."

Madame looked thoughtful. "That is very

kind. We are happy to accept this. Come along, Anton. We go talk to that *imbécile* at the desk now." She heaved herself to her feet and motioned to Anton to follow.

She paused by my chair to bestow a radiant smile on me. "You are a true gentleman. Thank you, *mon chevalier.*" She walked away, Anton tromping resentfully after her.

"Let's go home, Diesel." The cat popped out from under the chair before I could even stand.

At home we found the kitchen empty. Eschewing the wine, I opted instead for a gallon of my favorite chocolate chip ice cream. I sat at the table with a spoon and the untouched gallon bucket and enjoyed myself. I didn't eat the whole thing, maybe a third of it.

I felt better and guilty once I finished, but I ignored the guilt. Diesel had been in the utility room, and I could hear his munching sounds while I stuffed myself with chocolate chip ice cream. The cat came back to the kitchen, looking as satisfied and full as I felt.

My cell phone rang, and I pulled it out. Kanesha was calling me. I groaned, tempted to let it go to voice mail, but I knew I might as well talk to her and get it over with. I felt like a nap now, even though it was almost dinnertime.

"Hello. What's up?"

"I don't know whether to thank you or curse you," Kanesha said, a faint tinge of humor in her tone, "for sending Madame and Anton my way."

I resisted the urge to laugh. "I knew you needed to hear their story, and it was better coming straight from them."

"Yes, I'm sure you did," Kanesha retorted. "Talking to them was like trying to pin down Jell-O. But I finally managed to get the story out of them. Did you believe it?"

"If they told you what they told me," I said, "I believed part of it. Anton and Lombardi did have a loud argument. Laura heard them. Her dressing room was next to Lombardi's."

"Yes, she told me that. Also said she couldn't make out any of the words," Kanesha said. "So the only thing I have to go on with that argument is what Madame and Anton said. They even signed statements."

"It could be true," I said.

"I think the real reason for the argument is something else," Kanesha said. "I'm going to find out what it is. Do you have any bright ideas?"

I didn't think she meant to be offensive,

but I was a bit taken aback by the words *bright ideas* and her tone when she uttered them. "The main thing is to get on to Lombardi's lawyer. He's bound to know more about Madame and Anton than anyone else connected to the case. Madame says Lombardi left her all his money and his clothes to Anton, but Madame might have told me that to aggravate Anton."

"I've got a call into his office," Kanesha said. "He's somewhere in the desert around Palm Springs having a male-bonding experience, whatever that is. I'll try to get the details of the will from him when I talk to him."

"I'm sure you'll hear from him soon," I said. "In the meantime, have you thought about contacting the authorities in France?"

"The Sûreté, you mean? I've asked a contact in the MBI to do that for me."

The MBI was the Mississippi Bureau of Investigation, and I knew Kanesha had worked with them several times.

"I hope you'll get information from them," I said. "Did Anton happen to confess to the murder?"

"No, Madame said he would," Kanesha said. "But he called her an imbecile, and they argued about that for several minutes. Since he didn't confess, I saw no reason to arrest him." She paused. "For a nickel I would have arrested them both."

I had to laugh at that.

"If you tell anyone I said that," Kanesha said, "you won't be happy."

"I won't, I promise," I said, suppressing more laughter.

"I've got a call coming in on another line."

With that, the line went dead. She would be annoyed with herself for letting me see that human side of her, but I found it comforting. She kept her emotions so tightly reined in all the time, it was nice to hear her vent even a little.

I had barely put the phone down when it buzzed again. This time it was Melba. I hoped she was calling with information on Katrinka and her nephew, Micah.

Melba started talking right away. "Wait until you hear this. Have I got a scoop for you."

"I'm glad to hear it," I said. "So what's this scoop?"

"I was talking to Katrinka, like you wanted me to, and do you know what she told me?" Melba's voice held a note of triumph. "This is going to surprise you."

"Then surprise me already," I said.

"Katrinka's nephew, Micah, wrote that play," Melba replied. "Can you believe it?"

Twenty-Four

That, I had not expected. Was there a *third* Finnegan Zwake running around loose in this town? Or was he one of the two we already had?

"Is Katrinka's nephew Ulrich Zwingli Dingelbach?"

"Would you repeat that? Sounded garbled to me."

I took care to enunciate the words as clearly as I could. "Ulrich Zwingli Dingelbach. He's the author of the play. Don't you remember his father the history professor?"

"Yes, I do," Melba said, "but he can't be the author of the play. Micah Krause is."

"Was Micah going around disguised in a red wig and a bushy red mustache?"

"I don't know." Melba sounded subdued now. "Katrinka didn't say anything about that."

"Well, unless that was Micah in disguise, then we have three people who've claimed to be the playwright," I said. "And that's two too many."

"I suppose it could have been Micah dressed up like that," Melba replied. "Katrinka has told me he's basically really shy. He got started in acting classes to help him get over it, but she doesn't think they helped. Although when he gets onstage, he does well, like he did in that play I saw."

If Micah was really shy, then he could have been the Finnegan Zwake at the reception for Lombardi, I supposed. Then it dawned on me the reason he would have had for being in disguise. After what he had been through with Lombardi, he wouldn't have wanted the man to recognize him for fear of possible recriminations.

That might also explain his aunt's flirtatious behavior at the party. In case Lombardi did find out who Zwake really was, she might have been able to charm him out of doing something vindictive.

That made sense, but it didn't convince me that Micah was the true author of the play. Dingelbach had impressed me with his sincerity, and the fact that I had known his father swayed me more to his side. But was he simply pretending to be the writer?

"Charlie, are you still there?" Melba sounded aggravated now.

"Yes, I'm here," I said. "I was trying to process what you told me. Has either Katrinka or Micah talked to Kanesha? I think they should."

"They haven't, as far as I know. I've already told you that neither of them killed that actor," Melba said. "I know they had nothing to do with this."

I wasn't going to argue the point with her. "Let's forget that for the moment. Here's the situation. There are two young men, both claiming to be the playwright. Obviously one of them is lying. It could be important in solving the murder, and I think Kanesha needs to hear about this from Katrinka and Micah. Do you see my point?"

"Yes, I do," Melba said. "I'll call Katrinka back and tell her all this. If Micah really wrote that play, he deserves the credit for it. And if he didn't, well, I am going to have a lot to say to him *and* to Katrinka."

I started to reply but realized she had ended the call. I laid the phone aside. I thought I might be getting a headache. This investigation resembled a road up the side of a steep mountain, twisting, turning, with the occasional switchback or detour. I hated driving in such conditions, and I hated the frustrations brought on by this case.

I laughed, suddenly remembering Melba's

final remark. Katrinka and her nephew might find it a lot easier to talk to Kanesha than dealing with Melba when she got her dander up. One time — and one time only — I had incurred the Wrath of Melba, and that was a lifetime's worth of wrath in one go.

My mind reverted to the question of who wrote the play. I tried to recall what Frank and Laura had told me about Finnegan Zwake early on, and it wasn't much. I couldn't even be certain whether they told me they'd actually met him before all of this started.

I checked my watch. About to turn six. I called Frank's cell phone.

"Hi, Frank. How's it going?" I asked.

"Fine, Charlie. What's up?" he replied.

"If it's convenient for you and Laura, could I come over for little while to talk about things with you both?"

"Let me check with Laura," Frank said. He must have muted the phone because I couldn't hear anything for nearly a minute.

Laura spoke. "Dad, what is this about? You're not getting involved in the investigation, are you?"

"Not really," I said. "But I need to talk to you about the two Finn Zwakes. Look, it will be easier to do this in person. Can I come over?"

I thought Laura sighed into the phone. "Okay, Dad, come on over." The call ended.

Laura sounded annoyed with me, and I regretted that. I knew she was tired and stressed, but these questions had to be answered, and I wanted to ask them before Kanesha did.

"Come on, boy, we're going to see Laura and the baby."

Diesel beat me to the back door. He knew where he was going. Before I backed out of the garage, I remembered to text Stewart to let him know where Diesel and I would be for the next little while.

Frank let us in. "She's pretty stressed, just so you know."

"Thanks."

Diesel ran around the hall and then into the living room, searching for Laura and baby Charlie. Frank and I followed him, and there was Laura in her favorite chair, nursing the baby. The cat sat at her feet, watching intently.

"Hi, Dad. Come on in," Laura said. She sounded more her usual self. "Dinnertime for the little monster."

Frank and I took two chairs nearby.

"I'm sorry to intrude like this, but I need

to talk to you about Finnegan Zwake," I said.

"Which one?" Frank said in a wry tone. "Number one or number two?"

"I thought number one had disappeared," Laura said.

"He's resurfaced," I said. That caught their attention, as I thought it would.

"Where?" Frank asked.

"Turns out, he may be the nephew of one of Melba's friends. Remember the really attractive woman who caused the scene at the reception by flirting with Lombardi and getting Madame upset?"

They both nodded, and I continued. "She's Katrinka Krause. Melba took a trip to New York a few years ago to see Katrinka's nephew in a Broadway play. They went backstage after the play, and Katrinka and Melba met Lombardi."

"Let me guess," Laura said. "Luke made a pass at either Melba or her friend."

"Her friend," I said, "and she didn't like it. The nephew got involved, and Lombardi got him fired."

"So, is this nephew the first Finn Zwake?" Frank asked.

"Yes, and according to Melba, the real one, but I haven't seen any proof of that. His name is Micah Krause."

Frank frowned. "That name rings a bell. Where do I know it from?"

"Could he have been one of your students?" Laura asked. "Before I came along, that is."

"No, I don't think so."

"Someone you went to school with. Isn't he about your age?" I asked.

"Maybe, it's hard to tell. He didn't look familiar, but it was hard to see past that hair and the mustache," Frank said. "He could be anywhere from twenty-five to thirty-five."

"He already had a minor part in a Broadway play a few years ago," I reminded them.

"That doesn't help," Frank said. "Depending on the role, he could have been eighteen, and that would make him no more than, say, twenty-two now. I think Finn — the first one, that is — must be a little older."

"Forget about Micah Krause for a minute," I said. "Focus on him as Finn Zwake. How many times did you meet him in person?"

"Twice," Frank said promptly. "The second time was at the reception. The first time was about a week before, when I talked to him briefly in my office between classes. I really didn't have much of a chance to talk to him. The rest of the time we communicated via text."

"Did he ever say or do anything that would lead you to think he was a fake?" I asked.

"I don't think so," Frank said. "Laura, you talked to him once, didn't you?"

"Yes, on the phone, while you were in the shower, remember?" She raised her eyes from her son's head to look at me. "Frank's cell phone went off, and I answered without thinking. Finn identified himself, and we chatted a moment. I told him how much I loved the role I was going to play, and he seemed knowledgeable about it. He rang off before Frank got done in the shower. Said he'd text later."

"That's the only time you talked to him, other than at the reception?" I said, and Laura nodded.

"I know," Frank said. "There's an Internet database where you can look up people or productions on Broadway. Have you seen my laptop, honey?" He looked at Laura.

"It's probably in the same place it always is when you ask me that," Laura said.

Frank looked blank for a moment. Then he got up out of his chair and hurried out of the room.

Laura grinned at me. "It's on top of the washing machine. It's where he always leaves it."

"I found it," Frank called out from another room. "It was on the washing machine."

I laughed.

Frank returned with his laptop and dropped into his chair. He tapped keys for a moment, paused, then tapped again.

"Here it is," he said. "Micah Krause." He scanned his screen. "Born in Athena twenty-nine years ago. Bit parts in four plays, no lead roles."

"Is there a picture?" Laura asked.

"No," Frank said. He tapped his keys again. "Here's something. Looks like it came from the local paper about five years ago." He scanned the screen, then grunted. " 'Local Actor to Star in Broadway Play.' That's the headline. Whoever wrote this got a little carried away."

"Is there a picture this time?" I said.

"Yes, but it looks like maybe his senior class picture." Frank passed me the laptop, and I looked at the screen. The picture did look like a school photo. The Micah Krause in the shot wore heavy-framed glasses and had long, dark hair that hung around his face. He wore braces, too. I couldn't quite imagine this high school boy as the same person I had met in the red wig and mustache.

I handed the computer back to Frank.

"That's a terrible picture."

"Show me," Laura said. Frank took the laptop to her and let her see it. She giggled. "My goodness, that's awful. He looks like a nearsighted Afghan hound with bad teeth."

Frank took the laptop with him back to his chair.

I couldn't argue with my daughter, but it wasn't a kind description. "That was probably eleven or twelve years ago. He could have changed considerably in that time. Sean was still gangly and a bit spotty at that age himself."

"I remember," Laura said. "I'd never have believed, if you told me then, how handsome he'd turn out to be."

"Exactly." I turned to Frank. "Does any of this ring that bell any louder?"

"Yes." Frank nodded at the screen. "The second play he was in. I saw it in New York. I can't really remember him, because it was six years ago, and he had only a few lines. But I guess the name Micah Krause stuck in my brain somehow."

"Now that we've sorted that out, back to the main point of this conversation," I said. "Who wrote *Careless Whispers?* Micah Krause says he wrote it, and Ulrich Zwingli Dingelbach says he wrote it. Unless they collaborated on the play, which I don't think happened, one of them is lying. Which one? The pictures aren't helpful at all."

Frank tapped on his laptop again. "I'm looking up Dingelbach in this database. Let's see if he's in here." He shook his head. "I put in the full name, and no hits. Let me try just the last name." He typed again. After a moment, he smiled. "Now we're cooking."

"What did you find?" I asked.

Laura interrupted us. "I'm going to put the little guy to bed now. He's full and happy." She headed to the baby's room. Diesel accompanied her. He had to be sure the baby was okay. He would probably stay in baby Charlie's room until I was ready to leave.

Frank now answered me. "I found him under Ziggy Dingelbach."

"That's not quite as much of a mouthful," I said. "How old is he?"

"He's a year older than Micah Krause, and it says he's from Athena, so maybe they knew each other in school here."

"What credits does Ziggy Dingelbach have?"

"Only two, both bit parts from what I can tell. I'm not familiar with the plays." Frank paused. "One of them is a musical, so maybe he's a singer."

"Picture?" I asked.

"No, there don't seem to be many in this database," Frank replied. "I'll search his names on the Internet to see if I get any hits."

I waited, and Frank searched.

"Here's one thing, also from the local paper. Ziggy won a writing prize in high school, but it was for an essay. No picture." He set the laptop aside.

"I'm not sure we've made any real headway," I said, "other than that both of the Finns are from this area, are about the same age, and have had small roles on Broadway."

"That in itself is pretty amazing," Frank said. "Two young guys from the same small Mississippi town getting cast in shows? How on earth did they manage it?"

"I suppose they might have contacts in New York with some influence in the theatrical world," I said. "It's not unheard of."

"If they do, it would have to be someone from around here, or from somewhere in the state, I'd say," Frank replied. "Let me think about that."

I tried to recall the name of a Mississippi native who had made it to Broadway and was successful enough to get two young men parts in shows there. I came up empty, but it wasn't really my area of expertise. I had never seen a play on Broadway, whereas Frank had seen several and obviously knew much more about that milieu than I ever could.

"I'm coming up blank," Frank said after a couple of minutes. "I'll keep thinking about it, and maybe I'll turn up something."

Laura came back into the living room without the cat. "Diesel's on guard duty," she said as she resumed her seat.

"I figured he would be," I said.

"Did you solve any mysteries while I was out of the room?" she asked.

"We found Ziggy Dingelbach," Frank said. "He had parts in two plays on Broadway, and he won an essay prize in high school here."

"He has writing experience," Laura said. "But that doesn't mean he could write a play. I have to say, he was a lot more convincing to me. But if he's also an actor, he could be playing a part."

"Why? That's what I can't figure out," Frank said. "It's not like the play has been nominated for a Tony or a Pulitzer."

"I don't think we'll find out until we can get them both in a room together and ask them," I said.

"What if they wrote it together?" Laura asked. "Maybe they did, had some kind of falling-out, and now they're both claiming they wrote the play on their own."

TWENTY-FIVE

"I thought about that earlier," I said, "but then I dismissed the idea. Do you think that could be the answer?"

"Possible, and maybe even probable," Frank said.

"Thank you." Laura smiled sweetly. "I presume you're going to share this with Kanesha, Dad."

"Yes, I will. Katrinka and Micah, unless they want Melba to come down like the wolf on the fold, will be talking to Kanesha soon," I said.

"What are you talking about, *the wolf on the fold*?" Frank said.

"He's quoting Byron, I believe," Laura said. " 'The Destruction of Sennacherib.' Right, Dad?

"Yes. 'The Assyrian came down like the wolf on the fold,' and it goes on from there," I said. "In this case, Sennacherib was the Assyrian king who tried to take Jerusalem.

He failed."

"I wouldn't tell Melba you compared her to an Assyrian king," Frank said, "but I get your point. Melba will raise hell if her friend doesn't follow through."

"Yes," I said. "Now, I think it's time I left you and got back home. Thanks for letting me come over to talk about this. Things are perhaps slightly clearer now, but there's still a lot of fog on the road." I raised my voice a little and called my cat. A few seconds later, Diesel appeared. Many cats would have ignored such a summons.

I hugged Laura and patted Frank's arm before I left. Diesel wasn't happy leaving baby Charlie behind, but I got him into the car and drove home. I didn't feel particularly hungry, but I gave Diesel his usual portion of wet food for the evening before I headed up to bed.

Helen Louise called around nine while I was reading in bed. We chatted for fifteen minutes, not about the murder investigation by unspoken consent. After we finished the call, I was ready for lights out. Diesel already slept beside me.

In my dreams that night, I was being chased by two tall men in red wigs, both claiming to be Lord Byron. I woke up moments before I was ready to jump off a cliff to get away from them. I lay there for a few minutes, letting my breathing slow down, then got up and went to the bathroom.

What a strange dream, I thought as I got back in bed. I interpreted it to mean that my subconscious was still exercised by the two Finnegan Zwakes and sorting out which one actually wrote the play. Apparently my subconscious hadn't been paying attention when Laura made her suggestion that the two men had collaborated on the play. As I mulled the idea over again, I thought that Laura might have hit on the solution, or at least part of it.

I remembered then that I had forgotten to text Kanesha to say I had some information about both Micah Krause and Ulrich Dingelbach that could be useful. I glanced at the clock. Eleven seventeen.

What the heck? I picked up my phone and began composing a text to Kanesha. I stuck to the significant points. I told her about the Broadway database and suggested she look up both Micah Krause and Ziggy Dingelbach in it. I mentioned the photos Frank had found and shared Laura's idea that the two might have collaborated on the play. I sent the text and laid the phone aside.

A few minutes later, as I was drifting back toward sleep, the phone rang. I knew it would be Kanesha.

"Hello."

"I wouldn't have called this late, but since you were awake enough to text me, I figured you'd be awake enough to talk."

"Mostly," I said. "What's going on?"

"I talked to Ms. Krause and her nephew, Micah. Nephew stayed mum about Dingelbach, other than that he had met him a time or two in New York. Has no idea why Dingelbach claims he wrote the play."

"Is he able to provide any proof that he wrote it?" I asked.

"He gave me his agent's phone number. I'll call tomorrow and talk to her," Kanesha replied. "Do you have any idea where Dingelbach is staying? He's not registered at any of the hotels in town."

"No, sorry. Guess he must have friends or family here," I said.

"Perhaps," Kanesha said. "Well, that was it. Go back to sleep."

"Thanks. I will." I put the phone away and tried to relax again.

Where is Dingelbach? I wondered. Then I grinned. The question sounded like the title of a movie or a book. I pondered the question for a while until I felt drowsy enough to sleep.

I woke the next morning to find Ramses

purring and rubbing his head against my chin. I stroked his back, and he rolled over on my chest so I could scratch his stomach. Diesel meowed in annoyance and stuck his paw on my chest to stop me.

"Okay, you two, no fighting for my attention." I put Ramses beside Diesel and sat up on the edge of the bed. "Time to get up, I guess." I shambled into the bathroom and emerged shortly afterward with my robe on.

My bed was empty. The boys had relocated to the kitchen by now. I went downstairs and out the front door to retrieve the morning paper from Memphis.

I opened it on the way to the kitchen. As expected, one of the main headlines on the front page was about the murder of Luke Lombardi. Laura's name was mentioned as the costar, but to my thankful surprise, she was not named a suspect. I scanned the article, but there was no new information in it.

"Good morning, Azalea." I laid the paper on the table and took my seat. The housekeeper had already poured my coffee.

"Good morning," she replied. "I heard about what happened at that play. I thanked the Lord in church yesterday that Laura was spared. I also prayed that the evil man who did this would be found soon."

"Thank you for your prayers for Laura. I hope your prayers about the killer are answered soon," I said.

"They will be," Azalea said, serene in her convictions. "The Lord will shine the light when it's time."

I sipped my coffee and enjoyed the delicious scents coming from the stove. Bacon, hash browns, and scrambled eggs. I also detected the smell of biscuits in the oven. I did love my breakfast, especially the way Azalea served it. I reflected wryly that if she ever decided to retire, I'd probably lose ten pounds the first week.

The rest of the morning paper provided little of interest today. I sometimes wondered why I continued to subscribe, but the paper was part of my morning ritual. I didn't want to give it up. I supposed I was holding on to the vestiges of the print world. I still read mostly print books, and I stared at computer screens more than enough at both jobs, paid and volunteer.

Azalea interrupted these ruminations by setting a plate in front of me. I thanked her as always. She nodded her head in response. Diesel and Ramses appeared, one on either side of my chair. I wondered how much bacon Azalea had already given them before I got downstairs.

Ninety minutes later, having arrived at the library administration building, Diesel and I walked into Melba's office to wish her good morning.

She lavished attention on Diesel, barely acknowledging my presence. Not an unusual occurrence. My cat got far more attention than I did.

When Melba finally concluded her rhapsodies over my cat, she looked at me and smiled. "He's the best medicine. I feel even better now."

"I'm glad. It's good to see you back at work. Your friend and her nephew did talk to Kanesha yesterday."

"Katrinka called and talked to me about it afterward," Melba said. "She didn't say much, though, about what they told Kanesha."

"I heard from Kanesha last night. She told me a bit about the interview. All the nephew would say about Dingelbach is that he met him a time or two in New York. He says he has no idea why Dingelbach is claiming that he wrote the play and not Micah. Laura thinks it's possible they might have collaborated on it, had a falling-out, and now each one is trying to claim it as his work."

Melba looked thoughtful. "I wonder if Dingelbach is the boyfriend Katrinka mentioned one time."

"What do you mean? Micah's boyfriend?"

"Yes. Katrinka told me, maybe a couple of years ago, that Micah had called, all excited about this guy he'd met, and how they were so compatible. Both interested in the theater and all that kind of thing."

"Did he ever tell his aunt this boyfriend's name?" I asked.

"If he did, Katrinka never shared it with me." Melba grimaced. "I'm beginning to think Laura's right. I haven't seen Dingel-bach, though. Is he good-looking?"

"Yes, he's a nice-looking young man," I said. "This all fits, but maybe it's fitting a little too easily. Still, I'm going upstairs to text Kanesha about the boyfriend. I'll bet neither Katrinka nor Micah ever mentioned him."

"Why can't they just tell Kanesha the truth?" Melba burst out. "This is ridiculous. They're not killers. I simply don't believe they are, but I don't understand what they're trying to hide."

"I don't, either," I said. "When people hide things, it usually means they feel guilty about something they've done."

"Yeah, I guess you're right," Melba said. "I don't think they're guilty of murder, but there's something they're ashamed of."

"If you manage to get it out of Katrinka, you have to get her to talk to Kanesha about it," I said. "The more Kanesha can do to eliminate potential suspects, the faster she can hone in on the real killer. Kanesha isn't going to find proof of something that didn't happen, so if they're truly innocent, they don't have anything to worry about."

"That's good," Melba said. "I'll tell Katrinka that."

"Thanks. I'm going to head up to the office. Diesel, are you coming or staying with Melba?"

Thus appealed to, the cat looked back and forth between Melba and me a couple of times. He hadn't seen Melba in more than a week, so I wasn't surprised that he wanted to stay with her. When he was ready, he would come upstairs.

In the office I hung up my jacket and turned on my computer. When the latter was ready, I looked at my work e-mail. A couple of inquiries about items in the archive and one about a rare book. Answering them took only a few minutes. After that, I returned to processing a collection of letters written by a Civil War–era professor, donated to the archive by the man's great-great-granddaughter, now in her nineties.

I found such letters fascinating. The great-

great-grandfather had had a wide acquaintance and had apparently made copies of the letters he wrote, in exquisite copperplate writing. Filled with tidbits of daily life at Athena, and also opinions on the state of the country after the Civil War. Once they were ready for scholars to examine them, I would notify the appropriate person in the history department here.

Lost in the letters, I barely noticed when Diesel entered the office and jumped into his spot in the window embrasure behind me. A few minutes later my phone rang and jarred me out of the nineteenth century. *Kanesha.*

"Hello. How's the investigation coming along?" I asked.

"Not fast enough," Kanesha said. "I'm trying to find pictures of both Krause and Dingelbach. One of my men is over at the high school going through their collection of yearbooks. I'm sure the library must have copies of the college yearbooks. Are they in your area or in the main library?"

I felt such a fool. Why hadn't I thought about yearbooks? "They're here in the archive, and there's a set in the main library."

"Could you do me a favor and look through them? If you have time, that is. I

294

know you're at work."

"I can manage," I said. "I'll start right now, and I'll let you know if I find pictures of either of them."

"Thanks." She ended the call.

The yearbooks were in the room next to my office, the archive proper. "I'll be back in a minute," I told Diesel. He blinked at me and went back to sleep.

I unlocked the door and turned on the lights. First I checked the air conditioner and the air filter to make sure both were set correctly and functioning properly. The materials in the archive had to be kept at a certain temperate and humidity level. Both were at acceptable levels.

No one had asked to look at the collection of yearbooks here in the archive for years, thanks to the collection more easily available in the main library. At first I had trouble remembering where they were, but I soon found the shelf.

I had to take a moment to calculate backward, based on what I knew of the young men's ages, to decide which years to consult. If Dingelbach was thirty now, he would potentially have been a senior eight years ago. I found the appropriate year, turned to the section with class pictures, and scanned the names. I frowned. No

Dingelbach. I checked the other classes. No luck.

Then I remembered what Dingelbach had said, about his father dying fifteen years ago. Perhaps he and his mother had moved away, and he had gone to college elsewhere. I hoped the deputy going through the high school yearbooks had more luck.

Micah Krause was a year younger. I checked the juniors for his name, and I found him right away. The picture here wasn't much better than the one Frank had found on the Internet. Krause was still wearing the dark-rimmed glasses, and his hair was shorter, but it still framed his face in a way that semiobscured his features.

I checked the year after for his senior class portrait, and this one was far better. The hair had been cut much shorter, and the glasses were gone, perhaps replaced by contact lenses. Krause wasn't exactly handsome, but he had a pleasant face. I tried to imagine that face with bushy red hair and a big mustache. I was reasonably convinced that he was Finn Zwake the First.

On a whim, I turned back to the senior class portraits and began scanning the faces. When I got to the names beginning with an *H,* I found a face I recognized under the

name Jackson Arthur Howell III.
Alias Ulrich Zwingli Dingelbach.

Twenty-Six

Had I been a swearing man, I would have sworn over this latest discovery. This was absolutely nuts.

Why was Jackson Arthur Howell III pretending to be someone called Ulrich Zwingli Dingelbach? This made no sense to me, but I presume it must have to Howell-Dingelbach. I would have loved to get my hands on that young man and shake the truth out of him.

I turned off the lights and locked the door, taking the yearbook with me. I knew Kanesha wasn't going to be amused by this latest wrinkle in this already wrinkly case.

She answered my call right away. "What did you find?" she asked without preamble.

"I found out why you weren't able to find Dingelbach," I said. "There isn't any such person as Ulrich Zwingli Dingelbach. I found him in a yearbook from eight years ago under the name Jackson Arthur Howell the Third."

Kanesha did swear, and I didn't begrudge her. This was a frustrating twist.

"I also found a good picture of Micah Krause. I'd rather not release this copy of the yearbook from the archive, but you can probably get them to let you borrow the one at the main library," I said.

"Thanks. I'll send someone over right away. In the meantime, I'm going to track down Mr. Howell. Thanks, Charlie."

I started to say "You're welcome," but she was no longer there on the other end. I put my phone away and laid the yearbook on my desk. I called Melba on the office phone and asked her if she had time to come up for a few minutes to talk.

As I expected, she said she'd be right up. Less than a minute later, she stood in the doorway. I had heard her run up the stairs, and now she paused to catch her breath. "What's up?"

"Come on in and sit down before you keel over. Why on earth did you run upstairs?" I felt like fussing at her.

"Don't worry about that." Melba came forward and dropped into the chair in front of my desk. "I figured you must have hit on something really good. Otherwise you wouldn't have invited me up here. You would have just come down to my office."

"You're correct, as it happens." I brandished the yearbook and told her about Kanesha's call.

Melba leaned forward and practically snatched the book from my hands. "Why hadn't you thought of this already?" She started turning the pages.

I contemplated letting her scan through the yearbook until she got frustrated and gave up. She went to the junior class portraits, however, and found Micah Krause straightaway.

"Yes, that's Micah," she said. "He's not the handsomest boy in the class, but he is nice-looking." She glanced up at me. "Is that all?"

"No, look at the senior class. Find Jackson Arthur Howell the Third."

She shot me a puzzled look, but she followed my instruction. When she found the young man's portrait, she frowned at me. "So who is this?"

"That," I said, "is the young man who said his name is Ulrich Dingelbach."

"That's just plain idiotic," Melba said. "Why use an outlandish name like that when you have a perfectly good name like this?" She tapped the portrait with one finger.

"That's what I would like to know, and so would Kanesha."

"What on earth is he trying to hide?" She frowned, then suddenly stood and put the yearbook on my desk. She reached for the receiver of my office phone, picked it up, and punched in a number.

"Who are you calling?" I asked.

"Who do you think?" she retorted. After a brief pause, she spoke into the phone. "Katrinka, this is Melba. Does the name Jackson Arthur Howell the Third mean anything to you? Now, don't hem and haw on me. I want the truth, and I want it now." Melba listened for a moment and then nodded at me.

Evidently Katrinka was coming through with the truth. Otherwise I think Melba would have crawled through the telephone line and yanked the hair out of Katrinka's head. Melba angry was not a pleasant sight, and I was glad I was not the subject of her wrath.

Melba listened for another few seconds. "It's about time you showed some sense. If you know what's good for you, and for Micah, you'll get yourselves back over to the sheriff's department and tell Kanesha everything. You've both been acting like jackasses, and it's got to stop." She listened

301

briefly. "Okay, good. I'll talk to you later." She put down the phone and resumed her seat.

"Judging by your triumphant smile," I said, trying not to smile myself, "Katrinka told you what you wanted to know."

"She did," Melba said with an air of complacency. "That Howell boy was the boyfriend Micah was so crazy about, at least for a while. She swore up and down she and Micah would go and tell Kanesha everything."

"Good for you," I said. "I don't know if this information will crack the case, but it's time for these young men to stop playing games. Now that Kanesha has the name Howell, she can probably track him to one of the hotels in town."

"Maybe," Melba said. "That name sounds familiar to me." She thought for a moment. "Got it. Jackson Arthur Howell Junior used to be a CPA here in Athena, but he and his family moved away about five, six years ago. Maybe to Atlanta or Savannah, wherever his wife's family was from."

"I guess you didn't know them," I said.

Melba shook her head. "No, but a couple of my friends had him do their taxes. They said he was pretty sharp and got them more money back than they used to get."

"So you didn't know the son?"

She picked up the yearbook again and looked at the young man's portrait. "I probably saw him on campus," she said, "but that's all. Says here he got a degree in English. I knew more about the history department around that time."

I remembered she used to work for someone in the history department before she transferred to the library. That was before I moved back to Athena and reconnected with her.

Melba laid the yearbook on my desk again. "Was that everything?"

I had to laugh. "Yes, Agent Ninety-eight, that's all."

She grinned at me as she got up from her chair. "Then I guess I'll go back downstairs. See you later." She blew a kiss at Diesel, and he meowed to her.

I tried to focus on work after Melba left, but I couldn't stop thinking about the two young men who had claimed credit for the play. Was this a case of a relationship gone sour? Katrinka apparently said that Micah had been crazy about Jackson Howell, but that didn't mean they'd actually been involved with each other. It could have been one-sided, all on Micah's part.

If that were the case, however, why would

Jackson have been trying to horn in on Micah's play? What motive could he have if he hadn't had some part in the play's creation? Plain spite over a relationship gone wrong, perhaps? My continuing to speculate about this wouldn't get me anywhere. Only the two young men had the answers, and I doubted they would talk to me about it, either together or singly. Surely Kanesha, once she tracked down the errant Howell, would get them to tell the truth.

One question that really niggled at me was why young Howell had claimed his real name was Ulrich Zwingli Dingelbach. Why not use his own name? Frank had found Ziggy Dingelbach in that Broadway database, and he was apparently from Athena. Was it a stage name used by Howell? Perhaps his family didn't approve of his acting ambitions, so he didn't use the family name. But Ziggy Dingelbach?

It was certainly distinctive, I had to admit. Maybe there was already an actor named Jackson Howell or Arthur Howell. I searched the names, and variations of them, and found that there were actors under several of the combinations of the young man's full name. That would have been reason enough to use a stage name, but still, Ziggy Dingelbach?

This was really beginning to bug me. I hated unanswered questions, but I wasn't going to get those questions answered anytime soon unless I barged into Kanesha's office and demanded to know what she had found out. That wasn't going to happen. Kanesha would probably lock me up.

Focus on work, you idiot, I told myself.

Myself didn't want to hear that, but I did it anyway.

I managed to focus on work for about an hour, and Diesel slept in the window behind me. He woke, however, and evidently spotted squirrels or birds in the trees outside. He began muttering and chirping. He even pawed the glass as he sometimes did when he got really excited. I turned around to see what was capturing his interest.

Sure enough, there were two squirrels in the tree, apparently having an argument. Diesel itched to get at them, but I told him he couldn't. I knocked on the window, hoping the squirrels would hear me and be startled enough to go elsewhere. It didn't work at first, but I knocked again a few more times, and they finally got the message. They scampered down the tree and disappeared.

Diesel turned to glare at me, and he meowed loudly.

"Sorry, boy, but you were never going to get out there to go squirrel hunting, so you might as well calm down," I said.

A voice spoke from somewhere behind me. "Excuse me, but who are you talking to?"

Startled, I whirled around in my chair. A young man I suspected must be Micah Krause stood in the doorway.

"My cat." I moved aside so he could see Diesel in the window.

"That must be Diesel," Micah said as he advanced into the room. "Miss Melba talks about him a lot." He stopped in front of the desk and held out a hand.

I stood and shook his hand, and he introduced himself, an air of sheepishness in his demeanor. I indicated the chair in front of the desk, and he sat.

"I'm glad to meet you, the real you," I said in a bland tone. "What can I do for you?" I took careful note of his features, and I could see the resemblance to the Finn Zwake from the reception for Lombardi in the bone structure of his face and his eyes.

"I wanted to talk to you. My aunt doesn't know I'm here, and I managed to sneak past Miss Melba downstairs," he said.

"Why are you hiding from them?" I asked.

"Because they'll drag me back downtown

306

to talk to that deputy," he said. "She scares the heck out of me. The way she looks at you, you want to start confessing to all sorts of things you never even thought about doing."

I tried hard not to laugh. Kanesha could be intimidating, particularly to a young man who probably had little or no experience with law enforcement.

"I know what you mean," I said.

Diesel hopped down from the window and came to check out Micah. He held out his hand for the cat to sniff, and Diesel butted his head against the hand. Micah gave a couple of tentative strokes to the cat's head, and when he realized Diesel liked it, he scratched his head.

"Kanesha Berry can be extremely intimidating. I've experienced that myself, and I've known her for several years now," I said. "I also know that she's intelligent, competent, and fair. She isn't going to arrest anyone until she's certain that person is guilty. If you've done nothing wrong, such as murdering Luke Lombardi, then you have nothing to lose by telling her everything you know."

Micah grimaced at me. "Miss Melba said pretty much the same thing. She also told Aunt Kat and me about you and how you've helped solve some murders here."

"I have tried to help when I could," I said. "Kanesha isn't keen on my interference, as she often calls it, but I know I've been helpful in the past."

"Well, I need your help now," Micah said. "I'll go and talk to the deputy, but I'd really like to talk to you first."

Given my level of curiosity about this young man and Mr. Howell, I wasn't about to let this opportunity slip past. Kanesha would be peeved with me, probably, but I could deal with it.

"Okay, I'm listening."

Micah continued to pet Diesel, who was happy to let him do so.

"It's about Jack and me," Micah said, hesitantly.

I nodded encouragingly.

"I guess you figured out there isn't any real Ziggy Dingelbach," Micah said. "Jack made him up because there were already actors with names similar to his real one, and he needed a stage name."

"Yes, I had figured that out, but I have to say, he certainly picked a doozy." I smiled.

Micah smiled, too. "Yeah, it's pretty out there. His mom's uncle was a professor here at Athena. Taught history, and his name was Dingelbach."

"I took a class with him when I was a student here," I said. "I wondered if there was some kind of connection because he used the name Dingelbach."

"This great-uncle of Jack's didn't have any kids, and he was really fond of Jack. Gave him stuff, and took him on trips, but then he died when Jack was about fifteen. Anyway, Jack decided to use his name. It was his mother's maiden name anyway."

"That makes sense," I said. "I suppose you and Jack knew each other in college."

"Yes, sir, we did," Micah said. "We had some classes together, and we both acted in plays here. We were just friends then." He stopped suddenly, looking slightly embarrassed.

"It's okay. I understand," I said, and he smiled.

"Jack went to New York when he graduated. His parents didn't really approve, but they supported him. He was there a year before I went, and I roomed with him. And, well, things got pretty involved."

"You had a relationship," I said.

"We did, and for a while, everything was great. Jack's dad knew some people in New York, and one of them was a theatrical agent. She took Jack and me both on as clients. At first everything was perfect."

"What happened?"

Micah looked troubled. "Jack's a good-looking guy, and I'm only average. Plus, he can be kind of arrogant sometimes. He's an only child, and he's used to getting anything he wants."

I made a guess. "He wasn't getting the parts he wanted, and you managed to get roles in more plays than he did."

"Yeah, I don't exactly know why, but that's what happened."

"Did you ever consider that you might be a better actor than he is?"

Micah shrugged. "Maybe. The problem was, he auditioned for the same parts I did, and when I got picked, he didn't like it."

"Is that what led to the breakup?" I asked.

"Partly," Micah said. "We were both interested in writing, you see. I was always scribbling down ideas, and I used to talk to him about them. Then he tried to steal one of my plays."

TWENTY-SEVEN

"Was the play *Careless Whispers?*" I asked.
Micah shook his head. "No, this was a play I wrote before that one. It actually got produced, off-off-off-Broadway." He grinned. "Which means it was a low-budget production in a church basement."

I smiled. "But you had a play produced. That's an achievement to be proud of."

"Thank you, sir," Micah said. "I was proud of it. By that time Jack and I had broken up, and I had moved out of his apartment and found a place with three other guys."

"Did Jack have a copy of this play?" I asked.

"He did, but it was an earlier draft. When I moved out, I was upset and not thinking clearly. I didn't have that much stuff to move, but I managed to overlook a thumb drive. I still don't know where it was, but Jack found it after I moved out. He found a draft of this play on it. He tinkered with it and put his name on it and started trying to hawk it around."

"Why didn't he go through your agent?" I asked. "Did you both still have the same agent?"

"We did," Micah said, "and he didn't ask her to do it, because he knew she had already seen my version of it."

"Did he have any luck getting anyone interested?"

"Yes, sir, through his father's connection in New York. Problem was, the guy who was interested knew our mutual agent, and he talked to her about it. She recognized the play immediately and told him it was my play."

"What happened? Surely your agent wasn't happy with Jack over this?"

"She wasn't, and she threatened to fire him as a client. Jack somehow talked her out of it, apologized to her and to the producer. He can be really charming and very plausible when he wants to be." Micah sounded bitter, and I couldn't blame him. If he was telling me the truth, and I was reserving judgment on that. I wanted to hear Jack's version of all this before I made up my mind.

"When did all this happen?" I asked.

"About a year ago," Micah replied. "The other thing you need to know is that there was a version of *Careless Whispers* on that thumb drive, too. That's how he knows so much about the play."

I nodded. "Why the name Finnegan Zwake?"

"Jack suggested it. We'd both read the books when we were younger and thought they were awesome. We really got a kick out of the name. A lot of people don't get it. He said I should use a pseudonym until I was established as a playwright, since I had no real recognition as an actor. Made sense at the time." He shrugged.

Jack was beginning to sound like quite the manipulator to me. Getting Micah to use a pseudonym was clever. Jack could always maintain, with truth, that he came up with the name, and Micah used it, then tried to claim the plays that he, Jack, wrote. I wondered if Micah had cottoned on to this.

"He's a sneak, and a cheat, and I hate him," Micah said heatedly. "He's trying to steal my work, and I'd like to beat the crap out of him."

I understood his sentiments. Stealing another person's hard work was unforgivable. Whoever committed the theft in this case should be punished. I had to admit to myself that I liked Micah because he seemed genuinely upset. I reminded myself that he was actor, however, and I had to remain neutral for now.

"Have you talked to him since you've been in Athena?" I asked.

"No. I'm afraid I might start hitting him," Micah said with the ghost of a smile.

I nodded. "Okay, another question. The disguise you wore to the party for Lombardi at the hotel. Why?"

"I didn't want him to recognize me," Micah said. "He got me fired from the play we were in, just because I told him to leave Aunt Kat alone. He was an arrogant, pompous idiot, but he was getting rave reviews, and the producers wanted to keep him happy. So out I went."

"Did you think he would do something vindictive if he found out you wrote the play?"

"Yeah, I did. Probably foolish of me, but I was so excited about this production. I didn't want anything to go wrong, you see. I really believe in this play, and if it went over well with the audience here, it was a good step forward."

"It's an excellent play," I said. "I'm really sorry that you didn't get to see a complete production of it, but someone really wanted

Lombardi out of the picture."

"It wasn't me. I didn't like him because he was a creep," Micah said. "But he wasn't worth killing in my opinion. It must have been worth it to somebody, though."

"Yes, I guess it was," I replied. "Is there anything else you need to get off your chest?"

"No, I guess that's all," Micah said. "You understand the situation now, right?"

"I do, at least your part of it," I said. "You need to go straight to Kanesha Berry's office right now and tell all this to her. She'll have to verify things, of course, and she'll have to talk to Jack Howell. I told you she's fair, and I meant it. You have nothing to fear from her as long as you tell the truth." I hit those last three words with emphasis and watched Micah closely. He nodded.

"Thank you, sir." He rose from the chair after one last pat on Diesel's head. The fact that my cat had stayed with Micah the whole time we talked was a telling point for me. I wondered how Diesel would respond to Jack Howell.

Micah stuck out his hand, and I rose to shake it.

"I'm going to the sheriff's department right now," he said. "Aunt Kat is probably there already, and she'll read me the riot act

315

for disappearing on her. I just needed to talk to someone else, someone impartial, and I appreciate you listening to me."

"Good luck," I said.

Micah smiled and left the office. Diesel came back around my desk and leapt onto the windowsill. I turned my chair and regarded him fondly.

"He's a nice young man, isn't he?"

Diesel meowed. I patted his head and turned back to my work.

Micah Krause did seem like a nice young man. He came across as sincere and truthful. His story was plausible. I had known people like Jack Howell, or at least the Jack Howell Micah had described to me. I had little trouble believing that Jack, or even Micah himself, had done the things Micah ascribed to Jack.

One thing that weighed heavily in Micah's favor was Melba's assessment of him. She had always been a shrewd judge of character, except perhaps when it came to the men she dated. Otherwise she was hard to deceive. If she thought Micah was a good guy, then he probably was.

I still reserved final judgment, though.

I went back to work. Lunchtime would be here soon, and Diesel and I would head home for an hour before returning for the afternoon. I vowed I would concentrate on work until then.

I almost made it, but a nagging thought wouldn't leave me alone. Opportunity. Who'd had the opportunity to poison that bottle the night of the performance? And when was it done?

Motive was important, but without opportunity, motive wasn't enough. The prosecution would have to prove that the indicted person actually could have poisoned the liquid in the bottle.

What did the killer use?

Lombardi had died quickly, so whatever it was, it was potent. Cyanide in sufficient dosage killed quickly, but where would the killer have gotten it? Based on previous experience with a cyanide killing, I knew that it could be obtained over the Internet from outside this country. But the killer would have had to order it well in advance of using it. Did this mean the murder was premeditated and not opportunistic?

What role had the pranks played in this? Were they merely incidental, the work of someone else bent on annoying Lombardi? Or were they part of the killer's campaign against the actor? The first prank with the pig ears came off as juvenile, as did the snake in the dressing room. The hot pepper in the drink was more serious, but it wasn't on the level of murder by poison.

Another actor had been supposed to play the role, and Lombardi was enlisted only at the last minute, basically, because the original actor couldn't do the play. So that didn't allow for much premeditation, I thought. A horrible idea struck me. Perhaps the killer wanted to kill whoever played the part, so it was just Lombardi's bad luck that he got the role. If that was true, then I'd put my money on Jared Eckworth.

Surely Kanesha had talked to Frank about the mechanics of the production to work out when the poison could have been added to the bottle. He hadn't said anything about it to me, but neither he nor Laura wanted me to get involved in this case. I understood and appreciated their concerns, but they couldn't shield me from everything. My curiosity was an itch that never went away. Nor did my desire to protect my daughter or any member of my family.

By now it was time for lunch, so Diesel and I headed home. Azalea had baked a ham this morning, and I enjoyed a meal of sliced ham, creamed corn, and green beans, with a couple of slices of fresh, hot corn-bread with butter, topped off by a couple of glasses of cold iced tea. I felt like napping after I finished my meal, but I didn't have the time. While I ate, I decided I was going to head to the sheriff's department as soon as I finished my lunch. I would try to get in to see Kanesha and finagle some information out of her.

When I inquired at the front desk at the sheriff's department, the deputy on duty informed me that Kanesha was in her office. He would check to find out whether she could see me. Diesel and I went to the waiting area while he called.

We had to wait five minutes that seemed like fifteen, but Kanesha did consent to see me. Diesel and I knew our way, and we walked to her office.

"To what do I owe this visit?" Kanesha looked up from her desk, her expression enigmatic as ever.

I had decided to be honest. "Curiosity," I said. "I'm doing my best to keep out of your way. Given the fact that my daughter could easily have been killed Saturday night along with Lombardi, and that you were treating her as a suspect, I want this killer found as quickly as possible."

"I understand how you feel," Kanesha said. To my surprise, she followed that up with an invitation to take a seat. She even said hello to Diesel. He answered with a couple of chirps.

"What is it you want to know?" she asked.

"First, did Micah Krause come to you and tell you his story?"

"He did," she said. "He's plausible."

"What about Jackson Howell? Have you found him yet?"

"I did, and I've already talked to him."

I was happy to hear that. "What did you think of him?"

"Also plausible. In fact, he told much the same story as Mr. Krause, but with the roles somewhat reversed."

"Then he claimed that Micah stole his work," I said. "I guess I'm not surprised. Whom do you believe?"

"I'm inclined to believe Krause. I've met Howell's type before, and that type is smooth and very practiced at lying."

"I haven't talked to him since before the murder," I said. "He did seem completely honest when he explained why he was the author of the play." I hesitated. "But I found Micah Krause's version believable. Plus, Diesel really liked him."

Kanesha eyed me coolly. "He did, did he?"

Now I felt defensive. "Yes, he did. He's a pretty good judge of character. You should know that by now. I'll bet if he met Howell, he wouldn't like him."

Kanesha surprised me with her next comment. "You're probably right."

"Thank you." I suspected her of winding me up a bit, but that was okay. I risked another question. "Have you figured out yet who's guilty?"

"I have some ideas," Kanesha said, "but I have to have proof. I'm working on getting it."

I hoped she would say more, giving me a hint as to her chief suspect, but she didn't.

Try another question, I thought.

"Have you been able to find out anything about Anton and Delphine du Jardin?"

"I have, actually," Kanesha said. "I was able to get some information from France, thanks to my colleague at the MBI. The reason it didn't take long is because both of them have records there."

My jaw almost dropped. "Really? What for?"

"Petty larceny, mostly. Madame du Jardin likes taking things home from stores without paying for them, and Anton tries to pick up young men and women more than half his age. They've both served short terms in prison."

"How on earth did Lombardi get hooked up with them?" I asked.

"Not really sure about that, but they managed to get to New York about six years ago. Madame's mother was American by the way, so she can claim American citizenship. She and Anton are still married, too. They claim they're divorced, but we can't find any record of it."

"Fascinating," I said. "Were you able to find out anything about their history? Where they came from, for example?"

"A bit, though information on Madame is somewhat sketchy as to her past. Anton, on the other hand, is the son of a hero of the Resistance. No longer living, the father, but Anton managed to trade on his father's reputation in various ways until he started getting in trouble with the French police."

"Did you find out anything about their finances?"

"Not much. They don't seem to have any sources of income other than what Anton made working for Lombardi. Now that he's gone, I don't know what they're going to do for money. The French police are going to dig further, and maybe they'll turn up something," She paused. "And before you ask, I haven't been able to talk to Lombardi's lawyer yet. I also have a call in to his agent. Laura gave me the information. I should hear from both of them sometime today."

"I hope they can provide useful information," I said.

"Anything else?" Kanesha said. Her tone suggested that I had hit my limit on questions.

"What do you think killed Lombardi?"

Kanesha shrugged. "We won't have the tox report back for at least a week. My guess is cyanide, because he died so quickly."

"Were you able to get a sample from the bottle or from Laura's glass?"

"No, because they disappeared, presumably while everyone was focused on Lombardi there on the stage."

"What about the first time Lombardi's drink was doctored?"

"Same thing. Evidence disappeared during the confusion."

"Some little bee was busy," I said. "I'm sure you've talked to Frank about the staging and discussed who had the opportunities to doctor the bottle." She nodded, and I went on. "Have you considered a reconstruction of the murder?"

"Yes, I have. We're doing one later this afternoon, and before you ask, no, you are not invited. The only people involved will be Frank, his cast and crew, and my officers."

"What about the two authors and the du

Jardins?"

"They will be in the audience because I want all the cast and crew to have a good look at them. Maybe help stir up their memories." She glanced pointedly at a stack of files on her desk.

I stood, disappointed that I couldn't be present at the reconstruction. I didn't think even begging would sway her, so I simply said, "Thanks for the information. Diesel and I have to get back to the office."

She nodded in dismissal, and Diesel and I walked out of her office and down the hall.

A few minutes later, I was at my desk, with Diesel happy in the window, ready to nap. I appreciated the information that Kanesha had shared with me, but not being able to watch the reconstruction of the murder frustrated me. I felt like a child on the verge of a temper tantrum, and that was ridiculous.

Knowing Kanesha, she would have a guard posted at all the entrances to the building, and most of her men knew me, at least by sight, and they would be under strict orders not to admit me to the building. So there was no way I was going to get inside to see what took place.

Unless . . .

TWENTY-EIGHT

The more I considered my idea, the more excited I got. It could work. Now I felt like a mischievous child, determined to flout authority.

I stood abruptly. "Come on, Diesel. We're going home early today." Diesel complied with alacrity, and I shut down my computer and gathered my things. I hoped to get out of the building without Melba seeing us, because she would want to know why we were leaving early.

Luck was with me. Melba wasn't in her office, and Diesel and I made it outside and were off down the sidewalk, headed for home without anyone stopping us.

We reached home several minutes later, and we surprised Azalea and Ramses when Diesel and I walked into the kitchen.

Azalea gave a start. "What's wrong? Are you sick?"

"Nothing's wrong," I said. "I have a few

errands I need to run this afternoon, and I wanted to pick up a couple of things."

Ramses was climbing up my trousers, and he ended up on my shoulder, nuzzling my ear. That tickled, and I extracted him from my shoulder and held him to my chest for a moment. Diesel looked up at us and chirped.

"What do you need?" Azalea asked.

"I want to take a bottle of water with me," I said. "And a little snack."

Before I could get the items I wanted for myself, Azalea went to the cabinet and pulled out an aluminum bottle like the ones Stewart and Haskell took to the gym with them. She filled it with cold water from the fridge, handed it to me, and then picked up a couple of bananas.

"You probably want a candy bar, but these are better for you," she said.

I accepted them meekly and didn't argue. "Thank you. One other thing. Would you mind keeping Diesel here? And if I'm not home when you're ready to leave, Stewart will probably be here by then."

Azalea nodded, and I thanked her again. I had debated over taking Diesel with me, but he might draw the kind of attention I wanted to avoid if my scheme was going to succeed.

"Okay, boy, I've got to go, and you need to stay here, okay?"

Diesel didn't look happy with me, but he let me get out the door without vocal protest. I got in the car and headed back to campus. I parked in a lot not far from the lot near the performing arts building. I didn't want anyone to spot my car any closer to the building than this. I stuffed my bananas and my water bottle in my jacket pockets and locked the car.

When I reached the building, I tried one of the front doors. As I suspected it might be, it was unlocked. I opened it and stepped inside. I didn't see anyone, so I headed for the stairs that led to the balcony. My plan was to secrete myself there until Kanesha and the others arrived for the reconstruction. Then I could spy on them from the balcony. I doubted she would post an officer up there, so I should be safe from detection as long as I was careful.

I made it across the lobby to the stairs without meeting anyone. I scooted up the stairs as quietly as I could and emerged onto the balcony. I hung back to listen, but all remained quiet except the air-conditioning. The balcony was chilly, and I was thankful I had my jacket with me. The theater was dark, with only dim light emanating from the stage.

Now to find a place to hide until the reconstruction began. It was dark enough up here that I decided I ought to be safe if I sat in the corner seat on the highest row. There were floor-length curtains along the wall, and I could slip behind them if necessary. I checked my shoes. I had worn black ones today, and my clothes were dark, even my shirt.

I sat cautiously. Now that I had achieved my aim, I started thinking about what I was doing. I was flouting Kanesha's wishes, I knew. Normally I was a law-abiding citizen, but I felt that I had a stake in this case because my children were right in the middle of it. Perhaps I should have argued that point with Kanesha, and she might have allowed me to be here. I doubted Frank and Laura would have been happy with it, even if Kanesha had consented to my presence.

Was I here because I thought I might spot something that would help solve the case?

Probably.

Or was I here because I couldn't stand the thought of being left out?

Most likely.

I was here, and here I was going to stay until the reconstruction was over, or someone found me and kicked me out. That decided, I made myself comfortable and waited.

I dozed off. It was inevitable. The dark theater proved too much for me. I snapped awake, however, at the sound of voices. I sat up and looked down at the stage. More lights were on, but most of the theater remained in darkness.

Frank and Laura stood on the stage, along with Jared Eckworth and two other students. I couldn't remember whether they were cast or crew. Thanks to the excellent acoustics in the theater, I could hear most of what was said from up here, although microphones wouldn't have hurt. I doubted they would use mikes for this, though.

A quick check of my watch told me it was a few minutes before five. I decided to get behind the curtain in case they brought up all the houselights. If they did, I'd certainly be spotted where I was now.

The curtains contained plenty of dust, I discovered, and I shook some of it free when I moved the curtain. I could not allow myself to sneeze, and I tried to hold my breath until the dust settled. I couldn't stay behind this curtain for long, or my nose would start running, and the sneezes would most certainly follow.

I stuck my nose outside the curtain, but I discovered that I couldn't hear anything now. This wasn't going to work. I stuck my whole head out, and now I could hear. I would have to jerk my head back at the first sign of lighting on the balcony or the presence of someone else up here.

The voices continued, but the lighting hadn't changed after fifteen minutes. Then I heard Kanesha's voice, and I wanted to hear everything she said.

I slid down the wall until I was on my knees. I crawled out on all fours, head down, and made my way to the front of the balcony and the solid rail there. I had noticed gaps at certain intervals in the rail, and I should be able to look out through one of them and see what was going on.

I found the closest one and maneuvered myself into position. This meant lying on my side, my head on my arm under it. It wasn't particularly comfortable, but I didn't have a cushion to use instead of my arm.

Numerous people stood on the stage now, with Kanesha, Laura, and Frank in the center. I could see Madame, Anton, and the two Finns in the audience. Micah sat beside Madame with Anton on her other side. Jack Howell had opted to leave a seat between him and Anton. *A definite snub,* I thought.

While I watched, I never saw either of the young men attempt to speak to the other.

Frank called for attention, and all conversation ceased.

"Thank you," he said. "Here's what we're going to do. Basically, it's a run-through, and I want everyone to do exactly what they did on Saturday night. I know you might not remember every little thing, but do your best." He broke off because a hand had shot up.

"Yes, Jared, what is it?" Frank asked.

"Mr. Salisbury, who's going to take, um, you know, *his* part?" Jared sounded eager to me.

Frank disappointed him right away. "I am, Jared. I want you to do what you were doing Saturday, okay?"

"Yes, sir" was the sullen reply.

"We're going to do the first act, so everyone get in place. Chief Deputy Berry has a chart that was made from all our statements concerning our movements that night, and she's going to be checking it against what we do. Time to get ready." Frank waved the script he held, and the cast and crew dispersed to get ready. Once Frank and Laura were in their places, and the rest seemed set, Frank called out, "Curtain up."

That was the signal to start, and the run-through began.

Before long my arm started to go numb, and I had to change positions. I considered what to do. Thus far everyone's attention seemed focused on the stage, and I thought I might be able to peer over the balcony from a sitting position as long as I was careful. I rolled over on my stomach, waited until the feeling came back in my arm, then pushed myself slowly up onto my knees. I moved to the nearest seat and cautiously pulled myself into it.

Now I sat in the front row of the balcony in the last seat on this side. I hunched down in the seat a little. I could still see the stage fine, but there was less of me to spot in case anyone looked up.

After another fifteen minutes, I concluded that spying must have been pretty hard on the muscles, because my back was beginning to bother me from this hunched position. How did spies manage surveillance without crippling themselves?

Maybe they're younger and in better shape than you are. I hated that little voice of reason. I shifted cautiously to relieve some of the pressure on my back. I had begun to wonder why I was so eager to watch the reconstruction, because so far I hadn't learned a single thing of interest, other than that Frank was a good actor himself. He was simply more interested in the technical side of things.

Cast and crew reached the end of the first act, and Frank told everyone to come to the stage. "Deputy Berry has a few questions, I believe."

Kanesha rejoined them onstage. "Yes, I do." She turned to face the audience. "My first question is for Mr. du Jardin. According to your statement, you stood in the wings through the whole first act. Is that correct?"

"Yes, that is so. I watched in case my employer needed a quick repair or something else," Anton said.

"Thank you," Kanesha said. "Madame du Jardin, you were in the audience the whole time, I believe."

"Yes, I did not have a good seat, which was an outrage, you understand. Usually at all of Luc's performances, I have a good seat but not that night."

"That's too bad. You stayed in your seat during the performance, but did you go backstage during the intermission?"

"No, I did not." Madame sounded huffy. "Luc, he did not like me to. He had these superstitions like all people of the theater, and he would not allow me backstage until the end of the performance. You understand?"

"I suppose so," Kanesha said before she turned back to the group onstage. "I want all of you to think about these two statements. Who among you saw either Anton or Madame du Jardin during the first act that night?"

A couple of hands shot up. One of them belonged to Jared Eckworth.

"Yes, Mr. Eckworth," Kanesha said.

Jared stepped forward. "I was in the wings watching the whole first act, and I'm pretty sure Mr. Anton was there the whole time."

"Pretty sure?" Kanesha asked. "You aren't completely sure."

Jared appeared uncomfortable. "Well, if you must know, I was really nervous, and when I get nervous, I sometimes have to, well, you know, go to the bathroom."

"I see," Kanesha replied. "How many times did you go during the first act?"

"Only twice," Jared said, "and I wasn't gone longer than three minutes each time."

"Thank you, Mr. Eckworth. Now, who else held up a hand?"

A young woman stepped forward. "Emma Sprayberry, ma'am."

"Thank you, Ms. Sprayberry. What do you have to tell me?"

"I was in the wings, too, because I wanted to see everything. Jared is right. Mr. Anton was there most of the time, but a couple of times I looked over, and both of them were gone. Both Jared and Mr. Anton, I mean."

"Thank you." Kanesha turned back to the audience. "Mr. du Jardin? Would you care to amend your statement?"

Anton stood. "I did have to go to the restroom a couple of times, like Mr. Eckworth, but I did not think such a detail was important."

"Very well." Kanesha turned to address the group on the stage. A hand shot up. "Yes, what is it? And you are?"

A short young man with red hair stepped forward. He was frowning. "Tony Adams, ma'am. I just remembered something. I didn't think about it when I was talking to that deputy who interviewed me. I'm sorry. I guess I was stressed-out, but just now it came back to me."

"That's okay," Kanesha said. "That's why this process can be helpful. What is it that you remembered?"

Tony Adams hesitated; then he blurted out, "I had to go to the bathroom, too." His face reddened. "I had an upset stomach, and, well, I had to hurry. All I was thinking about was getting to the bathroom in time.

I remembered just now that I saw somebody near the prop room before I made it into the bathroom."

I held my breath. This could be it, the break that would solve the case.

"Who was it, Mr. Adams?" Kanesha's voice did not betray any emotion.

Adams took a deep breath, then let it out. "It was Jared."

Twenty-Nine

The reaction was immediate. All the young people onstage started moving away from Jared Eckworth as if they feared being contaminated by their nearness to him.

"Jared, what were you doing near the prop room?" Frank's voice lashed out, and the young man cringed.

Jared held up a shaky hand, almost in supplication; then his arm dropped. He stared at Frank in obvious terror. Frank approached him, and Jared flinched. Frank stopped a couple of feet away from him.

"Come on, Jared, tell me." Frank's voice had become gentler, coaxing. "Whatever it is, it's better to tell the truth."

Jared stared at him for a moment, then burst into tears. He covered his face with both hands and sobbed. Frank hesitated; then he put his arms around the young man and held him until the sobs ceased. No one in the theater moved. All eyes were riveted on Frank and Jared.

Frank stepped back and pulled a handkerchief from his jeans pocket. He handed it to Jared, and the young actor scrubbed his face with it. When he was done, he couldn't seem to decide what to do with it. He crumpled it up and held on to it, all the while the picture of abject misery.

"Okay, now, Jared. Tell me why you were near the prop room," Frank said. "We need to know the truth."

Words burst from him. "I didn't kill Mr. Lombardi. I swear I didn't." His chest heaved.

"What *did* you do, then?" Frank asked.

I had already guessed what he was going to say, and I was sure that Frank had, too.

"I played those jokes on him," Jared said. "The dead snake and the pepper in the tea. That was me. I really wanted to be the one to go onstage Saturday night."

"I see," Frank said. "You realize how wrong that was, don't you?"

Jared nodded. "I was an idiot."

"Did you plan to play another prank Saturday night? Was that why you were near the prop room when Tony was headed for the bathroom?"

Jared, looking even more miserable now, nodded again. "I was going to put more

338

pepper into the tea. I swear that was all. I wasn't going to poison him. I swear to God I wasn't."

Kanesha stepped forward. "Mr. Eckworth, did you manage to put the pepper into the bottle of tea Saturday night?"

"No, I couldn't," Jared said. "The room was locked. I didn't have an opportunity before, and I figured it would be unlocked like it had been the other time."

"Excuse me, ma'am." A slight young woman in jeans and a T-shirt raised her hand. She wore her thick blond hair wound around her head. I estimated that when she let it down it must have reached below her knees. "Jared couldn't have put anything in the bottle."

"How do you know that?" Kanesha asked. "What's your name?"

"Lexi Hollinsworth," she replied. "I know because I had the bottle with me. I was on the other side of the stage, and I had the bottle and the serving tray there waiting for the second act."

Another young woman spoke up then, and I recognized her as the actor who had played the maid. "Agnes Hankins, Ms. Berry. I saw the bottle and the tray right where Lexi said. I'm the maid in the play, and I was the one who brought it onstage."

"I don't remember any of this in your statements, Ms. Hollinsworth and Ms. Hankins," Kanesha said firmly. "Why is that?"

"Nobody asked me," Agnes said. And Lexi said, "Me, either."

Kanesha did not look pleased. "Someone was asked about the bottle during the interviews with cast and crew. I can't recall at the moment who that was."

Tony Adams spoke up. "It was me. I'm in charge of props, and Lexi is my assistant. I'm not sure why the bottle was already onstage. Before, we didn't put it out until the intermission. Mr. Lombardi insisted that the tea in it should be chilled and sweet. I kept it in a small fridge we have in the prop room. Lexi wasn't supposed to get it until intermission."

"Yes, that's true." Laura spoke for the first time. "Luke was very particular about not drinking anything warm onstage. He felt the heat of the lights, and he said having a cold drink helped his throat. I heard him explaining this to Tony the first day of rehearsals."

Kanesha nodded. "Why did you have the bottle already backstage, then, Ms. Hollinsworth?" Kanesha asked.

Lexi Hollinsworth seemed to shrink. "I didn't think it would really matter. I put

340

some more ice in it, and I figured it would stay cold enough. I had so much to do during the intermission, I thought it would save time. I didn't want to mess up and forget anything."

"This was Lexi's first time as a stagehand and props assistant," Frank said. "This doesn't excuse her from not following the directions she was given, but it's an understandable mistake."

Tony Adams scowled at the unfortunate young woman. "Your mistake made it easy for somebody to poison the tea, you know."

Lexi promptly burst into tears, and Laura went to her immediately.

Frank, his tone stern, reprimanded Tony. The props manager turned bright red again and muttered, "Sorry. Didn't mean to upset her."

Once Laura had managed to calm the girl, Kanesha spoke to her again. "Did you remain near the tray and the bottle while they were backstage?"

"Yes, ma'am, most of the time," Lexi said, her voice breaking. "I couldn't stay with it the whole time. I had things to do. I'm sorry."

"I understand," Kanesha said with more patience than I expected. "You were stressed, it was your first big production, and I'm sure you were nervous and fidgety, too. Am I right?"

Lexi nodded, and Kanesha continued. "Now, I want you to think carefully. You, too, Ms. Hankins. At any time while that bottle was backstage, did you ever see anyone else near it?"

"Nobody except Agnes," Lexi said.

"Nobody except Lexi," Agnes said almost simultaneously. Kanesha surveyed the cast and crew with a sweeping glance. "Anyone else notice anyone in that area?"

No one replied.

This was frustrating. The most likely time for the tea to have been poisoned was during the first act, it seemed, but apparently no one saw anyone near the bottle. But someone must have had the opportunity. Either Jared or even Anton during one of their so-called visits to the bathroom.

"Mr. Adams," Kanesha asked, "at any time before Ms. Hollinsworth brought the tea backstage, did anyone have an opportunity to doctor it?"

Tony shook his head. "After the first prank with the tea" — he threw a baleful look in Jared's direction — "I made sure the prop room was locked at all times when either me or Lexi wasn't there. We're the only ones with the keys, except for Mr. Salisbury."

"And surely the building custodian?" Kanesha said.

"Yes, that's correct," Frank said. "I had my key with me at all times."

"I think we need to talk to the custodian," Kanesha said, "but I'll get to that later. Now, Mr. Adams, tell me about making the tea."

Tony scratched his head. "Well, there's not much to it. We have a teakettle, and I boil the water and pour it over the tea bags in a pitcher, and then I fill the pitcher with ice. I add sugar, and that's it."

"You do this in the prop room?" Kanesha asked.

"Yes, ma'am," Tony replied. "There's a sink, too. That's where the water comes from."

Someone snickered, and Tony flushed red.

"Thank you, Mr. Adams. That's helpful," Kanesha said. "On Saturday night, when did you make the tea?"

"About half an hour before call time," Tony said. "Then I put it in the fridge in the prop room."

"Did anyone come into the room at any time when you were there?"

"Only Lexi," Tony said.

Kanesha nodded. "All right, I think that's

all. Mr. Salisbury, can I speak to you a moment?"

Frank joined Kanesha near the front of the stage, and they conversed in low tones for nearly two minutes. When they were done, Frank turned to address the cast and crew.

"I appreciate your time and patience, everyone. This has been really helpful to Chief Deputy Berry, and she thanks each and every one of you. You can all go now."

Frank waited a moment, then said, "Jared, I'd like to talk to you."

Jared came toward Frank, noticeably upset. I had observed that the other students had stayed away from him, and he had stood to one side like the pariah he must have felt he'd become since his confession. I had little sympathy for him. What he had done was nasty, and he could have badly injured Lombardi with his pepper trick.

I didn't think now that he had poisoned Lombardi on the fatal night. I believed he simply wanted to incapacitate the actor enough so that he could go on in his place. How he thought he'd get away with it on the night of the actual performance, I had no idea.

Kanesha joined the two men, and from the terrified expression Jared now wore,

Kanesha must have been telling him she wanted him to come to the sheriff's department to make a statement. I hoped this experience taught him that what he had done was inexcusable. I didn't think anyone would press charges, but his misdeeds wouldn't go unpunished by the college, I was sure.

The young people left the stage and, I presumed, the building. Jared wandered away on his own, his head down and his shoulders slumped. Laura and Frank left together, and soon only Kanesha and the four in the audience were left.

Jack Howell stood. "Can we go now? I don't know why we even had to be here in the first place."

"No, I want to talk to you and to Mr. Krause. Madame, you and Mr. du Jardin may leave. Mr. Howell, Mr. Krause, please join me onstage."

I wondered what Kanesha's plan was regarding the two claimants to authorship of the play. She had brought them together deliberately for a reason. Madame and Anton made their way to the front of the theater and disappeared from view. Madame, as usual, walked in front of Anton.

Micah and Jack made their way to the stage. Haskell had joined Kanesha onstage as well, and he pulled four chairs from the wings and placed them in the center, two facing two. Kanesha indicated that Micah and Jack should sit on one side together. She and Haskell took the other two chairs. Haskell had his notebook and pen at the ready.

Micah and Jack appeared to be studiously avoiding looking at each other. Jack tapped a foot on the floor, but Micah sat still, gazing into the space over Haskell's head, from what I could see.

"Now, Mr. Krause, Mr. Howell, I want to talk to you about the play. Before now, I've talked to you separately, and you both gave me similar stories. You've each claimed authorship of the play, and I want the truth. The college administrators are not happy over this situation, and they want a resolution, and so do I." She regarded them each in turn. I wished I could see her expression more clearly, but no doubt they were getting the full effect of her intensity.

Micah squirmed in the seat, but Jack lounged back in his, affecting nonchalance. His foot continued to tap the floor.

"I wrote the play," Micah said. "He can't stand it because I did better than he did in New York. I was in more plays, and I actually had a play produced. He couldn't handle it."

Jack uttered a scornful laugh. "You call those bit parts you had doing better? They were nothing, and you got fired from one of them."

"It had nothing to do with my acting," Micah said, still not looking at his former friend. "You know that. We were together when it happened, remember?"

"Yeah, I remember letting you mooch off of me, if that's what you mean." Jack sounded bored.

I disliked Jack's attitude. He was arrogant, and that made me like Micah even more. His personality seemed to have undergone quite a change since the first time I had encountered him.

"I spoke to your agent," Kanesha said. "I talked to her about both of you, and she shared some interesting facts. Would you care to hear them?"

I was watching Jack when Kanesha mentioned the agent, and he momentarily stiffened. He waved a hand. "Go ahead."

"All right," Kanesha said. "She told me that she had fired you as a client, Mr. Howell, because of your attitude. She said that when you did get a part, you argued with the director, the producer, and the other actors to the point that you got fired.

They labeled you as extremely difficult to work with."

"I can't help it if I have high standards." Jack sounded bored again. "You wouldn't believe all the substandard crap that goes on in New York and actually makes it to Broadway."

"Mr. Krause, on the other hand, was a pleasure to work with, or so producers and directors told her. He always knew his lines, took direction well, and got along with the other actors. I find that interesting."

Jack shrugged. "So they liked him. He was always a suck-up. What does this have to do with writing? I wasn't a good actor, so what? But I'm a good writer."

Micah laughed, and Jack rounded on him. He used a profanity, but Micah only laughed harder. Haskell got up and stood in front of Jack, the warning obvious. Howell subsided. Haskell went back to his chair.

Kanesha continued as if the interruption hadn't occurred. "I also talked to your agent about your writing. Again, she had interesting information for me. She told me you had both given her plays to read. She thought one of them showed a lot of promise." She paused a moment. "The other one, according to her, was juvenile and unoriginal, a thinly veiled version of an Ibsen play."

Micah laughed again. "You and your Ibsen," he said.

"I believe we can state with some authority that Mr. Krause is the true author of *Careless Whispers,*" Kanesha said. "In fact, your agent is willing to testify to that."

Jack stood abruptly. He yelled an obscenity and, before he could be stopped, ran off the stage and headed for the exit.

THIRTY

That puts an end to it, I thought. *Micah wrote the play.* I felt vindicated in my judgment of him.

Onstage, Micah stood along with Kanesha and Haskell. "I can't tell you how much I appreciate this, Deputy Berry. He's been a thorn in my side, and I couldn't get rid of him. You finally managed it, and I'm so grateful."

"All in a day's work, Mr. Krause." Kanesha shook his proffered hand. "You're free to go. You are not a suspect in this investigation any longer, and you may tell your aunt that she isn't, either."

"Thank you," Micah said. "She'll be as relieved as I am. Goodbye." He shook Haskell's hand, too, and then left the stage unhurried and no longer burdened by the perfidy of a former friend.

After Micah disappeared from sight, I hunkered down again, preparing to wait

350

until everyone else was gone.

"Charlie." Kanesha called out my name, and I nearly fell over, I was so stunned. I debated keeping still, but then I figured she would just come up here. How had she known? I had been so careful.

She called my name again before I could get upright. I popped up and stared down at her. Haskell was grinning, and Kanesha, from what I could see, was smirking.

"Meet us in the lobby," Kanesha said.

I took my time going downstairs, and I reached the lobby after they did. Haskell was still grinning, but Kanesha's expression had reverted to her usual enigmatic one.

"All right," I said. "How did you know I was up there? I was so sure no one could see me."

"I didn't *know* you'd be there, but I figured you'd be somewhere. The balcony was the only place that I didn't post one of my men. I figured you'd think of that, too." Kanesha's tone was cool, and I couldn't tell if she was truly angry or trying to wind me up.

"Well, if you wanted to make me feel like a fool, you succeeded," I said, slightly annoyed.

"That wasn't my intention," Kanesha said. "I didn't think it was a good idea for you to be here, but I figured you'd find some way to watch the reconstruction."

"Fair enough," I said. "Whatever you do, don't tell Frank and Laura that I was here. That goes for you, too, Haskell."

Haskell grinned at me. "Your secret is safe with me, Charlie."

"I won't tell," Kanesha said. "Now, let's all get out of here. I'm tired, and I want my dinner."

I thought about asking her if she had come to any conclusions after the reconstruction, but I decided I wouldn't press my luck just now. We parted ways outside, and I walked to my car and drove home.

I had found the reconstruction interesting, and it had cleared up some points. But it hadn't really solved the murder, unless I had missed something.

It did narrow the opportunity, however, I realized. That was important. If the tea had been kept under lock and key until Lexi brought it onstage, that meant it had to be poisoned while it sat backstage during the first act.

Who'd had the opportunity to poison it?

Everyone in the cast and crew, basically, as well as Anton, I realized. It would have easy for someone to pass by and drop something in the bottle. But was the bottle open?

I thought about that, recalling the two scenes I'd witnessed when Laura poured from the bottle. I didn't remember seeing her unscrew a top or pull a cork out. Kanesha would verify that with Tony and Lexi, and Laura, if necessary, but I thought the bottle must have been open and accessible backstage.

Opportunity established, now for motive. Who had wanted Lombardi dead?

Despite his claims of innocence in the poisoning, Jared Eckworth was probably still a viable suspect. I shouldn't ignore the fact that he was ambitious and he had some acting chops. That whole remorseful scene he enacted could have been just that, an act.

Then there was Anton. But what was his motive? According to Madame, Anton got nothing in Lombardi's will. She got it all, whatever there was to get. I doubted it would be a fortune. Lombardi had never made it to the front ranks in Hollywood or on Broadway, despite his one Tony-nominated role.

What about Jack Howell? Did he have any real reason to kill Lombardi? I suspected his only motive in all this was to persuade people that he had written the play. In his arrogance he perhaps thought he could cast Micah aside and claim all the credit for himself. His obvious bitterness over Micah's success, modest though it was, was a telling point. But I couldn't see that he had a strong, or believable, motive for killing Luke Lombardi.

Neither Frank nor Laura had killed Lombardi. Who else in the cast or crew could possibly have had a motive?

No one, I decided, unless there was a psychopath lurking among them. Someone who got the idea from Jared's pranks and decided to have a go at it.

Or maybe someone besides Jared who wanted him to be able to go on in Lombardi's place.

That was an interesting idea. Was someone in the cast or crew in love with Jared and willing to kill to help him get what he wanted?

That was a long shot, I knew, but it was within the realm of possibility. If anyone knew whether Jared had a secret admirer, Laura might.

When I got home, after receiving rapturous greetings from Ramses, enthusiastic ones from Diesel, and the usual from Stewart, I went to the den to call Laura.

"Hi, Dad," she said. "What's up?"

"I can't help thinking about the murder, and I want to ask you a question about something."

Laura sighed heavily into the phone, and I knew she did it for effect. "Yes, what is it?"

"It's about Jared Eckworth."

"I don't think I should be discussing my students with you," Laura said. "Even Jared, although I'm ready to kick him out of the theater department altogether."

"I know. Ordinarily I wouldn't ask, but this could be important."

"Go ahead and ask, and then I'll decided whether I can, or should, answer you," Laura said.

"Here goes," I said. "Are you aware of another student who might be romantically interested in Jared?"

"That's an odd question," Laura said. "Why would you ever want to know such a thing?"

I repeated my statement about the potential importance.

"All right," Laura said. "Yes, there is someone who I think is nursing a big crush on Jared. You don't know her, unless you remember her from the play. Her name is Lexi Hollinsworth, and she's assistant props manager."

Lexi Hollinsworth, who had stayed near

the bottle of tea during the first act, had a crush on Jared. Could Lexi be the killer?

"Would you say Lexi is a well-balanced individual?" I asked, trying for a casual tone.

"Dad, this is really a bit much. I'm not a psychologist," Laura said.

"I know I'm asking a lot, sweetheart, but I swear there's a good reason for these questions."

There was silence at the other end; then Laura said, "Oh, my Lord, Dad. You think Lexi might have poisoned Luke because she's so in love with Jared that she would kill for him. Just so he could have his time onstage."

"Yes, basically. I think it's a possibility, but I don't know the girl. Jared could also have asked her to do it for him, telling her it was just a prank again. She knows now it wasn't, but she's protecting him."

"I think you've gone too far, Dad." Laura didn't sound angry. "Lexi is a nice girl, quiet, respectful, not one of my best students, but a good one. She does have a thing for Jared. I've caught her staring at him in class when she should be paying attention. But that doesn't make her a killer."

"I agree," I said. "But it is just possible. Kanesha will have to sort it out."

"You're really going to share this theory

with Kanesha?" Laura sounded peeved now. "Dad, I wish you would just leave it alone."

"I can't," I said flatly. "You could have been killed as well, Laura, and I can't and won't forget that. The person who did this to Lombardi has to be caught."

"All right, you've made a good point," Laura said. "I can't argue with you, and I'm not sure I want to now. I guess I can understand why you can't just let it go. Talk to Kanesha if you have to."

"Thank you, sweetheart," I said. There were many things I could have said to her then, but I didn't want both of us crying on the phone.

Laura understood. "I love you, too, Dad."

We bade each other good night, and I put my phone down for a moment. I tried to collect my thoughts before I chatted to Kanesha. I knew this was a long shot, but even if it turned out to be a false trail, I felt it had to be explored to make sure.

I decided to text Kanesha rather than call. She preferred a text message. It was better to let her call me when she was ready to talk to me. Or *deal with me,* as she might have phrased it.

Have information about Jared and Lexi Hollinsworth. Could be really important.

That should have sufficed. No need to go

into detail in a text message. I had no idea when she might call or text back, so I headed for the kitchen. I had never eaten my bananas or drunk the water. In fact, they were still in my jacket pockets. The bananas, I discovered, were not in good condition, and I would have to take the jacket to the cleaners in hopes they could get rid of the mushed banana stains. The water was luke-warm now, but I set the bottle in the fridge rather than pour it out.

"What on earth were you doing?" Stewart had been observing me with a quizzical expression. "Rolling around on the floor with bananas in your pockets?"

That was too close to the truth for comfort. I shrugged. "Sort of. I'll tell you about it later, okay?"

"Sure," Stewart said. "You missed dinner, but Azalea put a plate together and left it in the oven for you."

"What time is it?" I had completely lost track and hadn't even checked when I texted Kanesha.

"Seven seventeen," Stewart said. "You didn't eat out, did you?"

"No." I extracted the plate from the oven and tested the heat level. Everything seemed warm enough to eat. There was chicken cas-serole and English peas and two of Azalea's homemade yeast rolls.

"There's also salad in the fridge," Stewart said. "Would you like some?"

"No, this is fine." When I took my seat at the table, I had three four-legged friends, two feline, one canine, interested in what I was doing.

Stewart laughed. "Don't be suckered in. They've all had plenty to eat."

"That never stops them, though." I started on the chicken casserole.

"Dante, come over here and leave Charlie alone," Stewart said in a tone of command. Dante minded, because he knew that tone.

That left me with Diesel and Ramses on either side of my chair. "Look, boys, you're not getting anything, so just sit there and be good while I eat, okay?"

Diesel meowed, but Ramses squeaked at me in protest. "No," I said in a firm voice. Ramses squeaked again, but not as loud. I ignored him and devoted myself to my food.

I was so lost in thought that I wasn't paying any attention to Stewart. Eventually he called my name, and when I looked at him, he said, "Where are you, Charlie? What's going on?"

I felt the urge to confess to him. I knew he would not tell Frank or Laura if I asked him not to. Haskell might tell him I was there at the reconstruction, but he might not. I decided to bare all after first swearing him to secrecy.

"I promise I won't breathe a word, even to Haskell," Stewart said. "What did you do?"

"All right, I'll tell you, but no joking about it."

Stewart nodded. "Scout's honor."

I told him about the reconstruction while I finished my meal, and Stewart listened avidly until I was done.

"Who do you think did it?"

"I have this wild theory. You might laugh, but I'll tell you anyway."

"I won't laugh. Get on with it."

"It's two of the students, Jared Eckworth and Lexi Hollinsworth. Jared confessed to the first two pranks, as I told you. I talked to Laura, and she says Lexi has a big crush on Jared. I thought it was possible that she either decided to remove Lombardi so Jared could get his chance or maybe Jared persuaded her to put the poison in the bottle for him, not knowing he intended to kill Lombardi. And now she's protecting him."

"Lexi Hollinsworth, you said." Stewart looked thoughtful. "She's a chemistry major. Did you know that?"

THIRTY-ONE

"No, I didn't know that. Do you think she has the skills and the knowledge to make poison — say cyanide, for example?" I asked.

"Yes, she's a fantastic student," Stewart said. "Her lab work is excellent, and the information is easily available. I can check the logs in the department. We keep track of every chemical and who uses what."

"Let me talk to Kanesha first," I said. "She might not find it necessary."

"Sure," Stewart said. "I think this is a long shot, as you said, but it's just possible, I suppose."

"She had the best opportunity," I said. "I think the case hinges on that."

"If you're right, and Kanesha can prove it, then it's done," Stewart said. "We're all ready for this to be over."

"Amen," I said.

Stewart got up from the table and pointed

to my empty plate. "Would you like more? It won't take a minute or two in the microwave, and there's plenty left over."

I hesitated. "I wouldn't mind another helping of the casserole and another roll."

"Coming up," Stewart said as he collected my plate.

"Thank you," I said, feeling a bit guilty letting him wait on me.

"Not a problem," he said.

When the food was ready, he set the plate in front of me again. "Enjoy."

I nodded. I slathered the roll with butter and started on the casserole. Diesel and Ramses hadn't given up yet, but I paid them no attention. There were times I regretted ever letting them have people food, and this was one of them.

When I finished, I decided to relent a little and let each of them lick my fingers, buttery from the dripping roll. That seemed to satisfy them.

I got up to wash my hands and to put the plate and utensils in the dishwasher.

"Do you think Kanesha is going to call you back?" Stewart set his own phone on the table and regarded me.

"I never know with her. She might not call me at all, or she could call me at midnight.

I wonder sometimes how much she actually sleeps."

"She's pretty driven when she's working a case. That's the word Haskell used when he talked to me about her once. She feels like she has to be three times as good as anyone else because of her gender and her race."

"Sad to say, but she's probably right," I said. "There's no denying that she's smart, capable, and full of integrity."

"I agree. That's why Haskell is so devoted to her. She is everything he admires most in a cop. I think he's smart, capable, and full of integrity, too."

"I wouldn't argue with you on that," I said. "He's a good man."

"The best," Stewart said simply. His phone rang. "Speak of a handsome devil. Excuse me while I take this." He picked up the phone and left the room.

I stared at my phone. "Okay, it's your turn to ring, darn it. Ring."

The phone didn't respond.

I was tempted to look in the fridge for some kind of dessert. I knew I would find something, but I remembered the third roll and the second helping of casserole. I would skip dessert, at least for now. Later, well, maybe.

I decided to go upstairs and change out of

my soiled clothes. I left the jacket on the coatrack in the hall as a reminder to myself to take it to the cleaners. Diesel and Ramses raced up the stairs ahead of me. I made it halfway up before I remembered that I had left my phone on the kitchen table. I thought about leaving it, but I was sure if I did, Kanesha would call while I was upstairs. I went back down and retrieved the phone, then once more headed up the stairs.

A quarter hour later, attired in more comfortable clothing, namely a T-shirt and sweatpants, I went back downstairs to the den and prepared to relax in the recliner with the television. I had hoped to hear from Helen Louise by now, but she hadn't called. Busy at the bistro, as usual.

Ramses hopped into my lap, and Diesel got comfortable on the sofa. I switched the TV on. It was still set to the same channel, and I didn't change it. I put my phone on the arm of the chair and tried to relax.

I had the feeling that the end was in sight, and I was anxious for this all to be over. I wouldn't be able to relax completely until the killer had been arrested, but I had to work out some of the tension somehow. I forced myself to pay attention to the sitcom, and I was able to get involved in it for a few minutes. Then a commercial came on, for home security of all things, and I felt my anxiety return.

At this rate, I was going to have to take something to help me sleep tonight. When I got like this, I had trouble nodding off. I hadn't been this worked up by any of the investigations in which I'd taken part, but this one hit even closer to home than any of the others. I no longer thought that Laura was in any danger. That had been a bit irrational on my part, but the anxiety was hard to shake.

Why doesn't Kanesha call?

Maybe she had already made an arrest, and if so, she had no reason to inform me right away. She might have called Frank and Laura, though, and one of them would surely call me in that case.

More likely, I thought, she was waiting for more information. She hadn't mentioned anything about having talked to Lombardi's lawyer, and he could have key information about Lombardi's estate. If Madame was wrong about the will, and Anton was due to receive a large sum of money, that would give the dresser a strong motive.

I thought Madame was a mercenary creature at heart who had latched on to Lombardi because of his measure of notoriety and his potential to make a lot of money if he ever hit it big. Perhaps she had grown tired of him, however, and was ready to get rid of him and inherit whatever he had willed to her. She hadn't had the opportunity to poison Lombardi, of course, but might she have talked Anton into it? She treated him badly, but he wouldn't have put up with it if he didn't expect something from her, surely.

Why hadn't I thought about Madame before? Because she wasn't present on the stage when the poison was likely added to the tea. Also because she hadn't been in the theater, to my knowledge, when the pranks had been played on Lombardi. For example, where would she have found a snake? I couldn't see her as being willing to handle one, but again, she might have persuaded Anton to do it.

Jared had confessed to being the prankster now so that absolved Madame of possible guilt. I thought there was still a possibility that she could have talked Anton into killing Lombardi with the promise of financial rewards. Anton, Lexi, and Jared all had had the opportunity, but which had had the most compelling motive that pushed him or her to kill?

I looked at the time on my phone. Going

on eight forty-five. Earlier than usual for me to go to bed, but the way I felt now, I might as well.

"Come on, boys, we're going up to bed." I put the footrest down and set Ramses on the floor. Diesel knew the word *bed,* and I had begun to suspect that Ramses did, too. They were well ahead of me by the time I got to the stairs. Stewart wasn't in the kitchen, so I headed upstairs, leaving lights on for Haskell.

In my bathroom I found the sleep aid I used at times like this and swallowed it with water. It usually took about half an hour to put me to sleep. The boys waited for me in the bed, and I pulled back the sheets and slipped in next to them. My phone was on the bedside table, and I turned the light off.

My mind kept going from idea to idea in a relentless kind of hopscotch as I considered the possibilities. Jared? Lexi? Anton? Which one of them had done it? Or was there someone I had missed completely? Perhaps Kanesha knew a lot more than I did and had other suspects in mind.

This went on until I began to feel drowsy. My phone hadn't rung, and at some point, I fell asleep with Diesel by my side and Ramses on my chest.

Whatever I dreamed during the night was

gone by the time I woke up around five that morning. I had slept soundly, and other than a slight hangover from the drug, I felt good. I picked up my phone and checked for any calls or texts I might have missed. Not a single one, not even from Helen Louise. That really disappointed me. Why hadn't she called?

To be fair, even if she had, I might not have heard the phone, I realized, so I couldn't be too annoyed with her. I thought about staying in bed, but I knew I'd lie there, awake, when I could be up and doing something. My restless energy of the previous evening had come back.

I got up and put on my bathrobe and slippers and picked up my phone. Diesel and Ramses raced down ahead of me. I fed them right after I turned on the coffeemaker, set up by Stewart last night. I went to retrieve the paper. It was still dark outside, and would be for a good hour yet, and it took me a minute to locate the paper.

Back in the kitchen I took my place at the table and spread out the paper. The local murder no longer rated space on the front page, evidently. I scanned the headlines, but none drew me in. I looked through more of the paper, but I couldn't even focus on the comic strips that I usually enjoyed.

By now the coffee was ready, and I poured myself a mug. Perhaps caffeine would help me settle down and focus. Oddly enough, it often did. Maybe some of my jitters this morning came from caffeine withdrawal.

Diesel had been playing with Ramses but perhaps had had enough. He came to sprawl on the floor by my chair and nap. Ramses continued to run around the kitchen, chasing an imaginary bug. At least I hoped it was imaginary. I couldn't see anything on the floor.

For some reason Anton was on my mind, and I tried to recall what Kanesha had shared with me about him. One of the details that had interested me at the time was the fact that Anton's father had been a hero of the French Resistance. I was curious about him, so I used my phone to find information. I didn't know his name, other than his surname, so I searched for *French Resistance hero du Jardin*.

I got immediate results. I clicked on the link to what looked like a reputable website with a biography in English. I skimmed through the somewhat lengthy entry, picking out the details. Antoine Justin du Jardin had indeed been a hero. His list of escapades was long, and the fact that he had eluded the Nazis several times was greatly to his credit. Some of his comrades had not been so lucky, but each of them had had a cyanide capsule to take if necessary. Obviously du Jardin had not needed his. He seemed to have been a genius at escaping traps.

I put my phone down and sipped at my coffee. What must it have been like, growing up with a father like that? A national hero, celebrated for his acts of bravery. Must have been hard on a kid like Anton.

I thought about the elder du Jardin's less fortunate colleagues. I wondered how many had used their cyanide pills to avoid Nazi torture and murder.

That sparked a line of thought that was intriguing. My phone rang and interrupted it.

Kanesha had finally called.

"Good morning," I said. "What did you think of my text?"

"Interesting," she replied. "I called to tell you about something that happened during the night. Someone attacked Lexi Hollinsworth pretty brutally. She's in the hospital in a coma now."

Thirty-Two

For a moment I was too stunned to say anything. That poor young woman.

"Will she recover?" I asked.

"A little early to tell," Kanesha said. "Her doctor is hopeful because she's young and in good shape physically, but she sustained a lot of damage."

"Why would anyone attack her?" I asked, still trying to come to grips with this horrible news.

"That's what I intend to find out," Kanesha said, her tone sharp.

"When did it happen?"

"Last night around eleven," Kanesha said. "She stayed late to study in the library at the college, and she walked home from there. She rents a garage apartment about six blocks from campus. Her attacker followed her and caught up with her in front of the house where her apartment is located. He hit her multiple times with something like a tire iron or a baseball bat. The only reason the attacker didn't kill her is that her landlord was up watching television and heard her scream. He's elderly, but he's a veteran and tough. He charged out of the front door yelling, and the attacker ran off."

I felt sick to my stomach. The cold-bloodedness of this act frightened me. "Was he able to give any sort of description?"

"Nothing that's really helpful," Kanesha replied. "He said the attacker was hunched over when he ran out the door yelling, and the guy scuttled away. He was wearing dark clothing, of course, and had something over his face."

"So no real clues to his identity," I said.

"No," Kanesha replied. "Right now I'm working on finding out where certain persons were during the time the attack took place."

"Would those certain persons be Jared Eckworth and Anton du Jardin?" I asked.

"Among others," Kanesha replied. "What is this interesting information you wanted to share with me?"

I told her what Laura had said about Lexi Hollinsworth having a crush on Jared and that I thought it possible she might have been tricked into poisoning the tea by Jared or had done it herself for Jared's sake.

"She's a chemistry major, according to Stewart, and he says she's excellent at lab work."

"So she could have made the poison herself," Kanesha said. "That is interesting. I'll have to ask the chemistry department to find out what she has been working on. This could be why her attacker wanted her dead."

"I'll be praying that she comes out of her coma and can tell you what she knows. She may have recognized her attacker."

"It's possible," Kanesha said, "but I can't wait for her to wake up. I want this guy stopped immediately. I'll talk to you later."

I put my phone down, still shaken by the news. The fact that Lexi was attacked strengthened my conviction that I was right about what had happened. She had poisoned the tea, but whether on her own or egged on by Jared was the question. The fact that she had been attacked led me to believe that Jared was responsible. He had talked her into adding the poison to the tea, and now he was terrified that she would tell Kanesha what she had done and why.

How was Kanesha going to find the evidence to prove this, if Lexi Hollinsworth was unable to talk?

I felt sure Jared wouldn't have an alibi for the time in question. Kanesha could pull him in to be questioned, and maybe he would confess. Then this nightmare would be over, but not for poor Lexi.

Azalea would be here soon, I knew, and her presence would be more welcome than ever. I still felt a bit sick over the news about Lexi Hollinsworth, and I wished I could do something to help her heal. What I could do was pray, and that is what I did, as fervently as I knew how.

I hadn't thought to ask Kanesha whether Lexi had any family. I knew they would be notified, if they existed, and I could only imagine how shocked they would be. This was beyond a nightmare for any parent to receive such news.

My phone rang, and I saw that Laura was calling. I wondered if she had heard the news about Lexi. The moment she spoke, I knew she had.

"Hello, Dad. Have you heard?"

"Yes, sweetheart, I have. Kanesha called me a couple of minutes ago."

"She called us earlier to find out whether we knew anything about Lexi's family." Her voice caught on a sob. "Why would anyone do this to her? I just don't understand."

"To keep her from talking to Kanesha," I said. "Lexi must know something, or she wouldn't have been attacked."

Laura didn't respond for several seconds, and I knew she was processing the statement. "So you think Jared did this?"

"I think he's the most likely person."

"Because she knows he killed Luke?"

"Possibly," I said. "Also, Jared could have talked her into putting something into the tea and told her it was just a prank. Then, when Luke died, she was afraid to say anything because she didn't want to get into trouble or get Jared into trouble."

"I can't believe this," Laura said. "Jared has always seemed like such a nice young man. I've known he was ambitious, but this is insane. If he killed Luke, what did he possibly think he would gain?"

I reminded her that Miss An'gel had hoped to bring her New York director friend down to see the play.

"Even so, Dad, that's such a long shot. Jared isn't stupid. Frank and I both stress to our students, over and over again, how difficult a profession acting is. How many good actors end up in New York or L.A. and never make it."

"What's that quotation from *Macbeth,* you know, from early in the first act? About ambition?" I asked.

After a brief hesitation, Laura quoted it.

I have no spur
To prick the sides of my intent, but only
Vaulting ambition, which o'erleaps itself,
And falls on th'other. . . .

"Vaulting ambition," I said. "Think of Macbeth and, of course, Lady Macbeth."

"I see your point, and it's a valid one. A truly ambitious person can be extremely ruthless," Laura said, now sounding depressed. "I find it hard to see Jared that way. I know how eager he is, because he is truly talented and could go far, if he gets the right breaks."

" 'One may smile, and smile, and be a villain.' "

Laura sighed again. "Yes. *Hamlet.* I know, Dad. This is hard for me, and I think Frank will probably feel the same way about a student he's worked with and one he sees as having so much promise."

"I'm sorry, sweetheart. I hope for your sakes that Jared isn't the killer, but someone has to be. At this point the field has narrowed considerably." I almost gave myself away then by saying something about yesterday's reconstruction, but I caught myself in time.

"The reconstruction yesterday confirmed that, all right. We found out that the poison could only have been put in the tea during the first act, because Lexi had brought it backstage to save time, instead of waiting to get it during the intermission."

"Wouldn't a lot of people have been hanging around in the wings?" I began to rue my deception more and more. After the case was over and done with, I could confess to Laura and Frank. At the moment, I didn't want to upset them any more than they already were.

"Yes, but Lexi claimed that either she or Agnes, the actor who played the maid, was near the bottle during the first act. Neither one of them could recall seeing anyone else near it."

"Then either Lexi or Agnes is the most likely person to have done it, if that's true. What about during the intermission? Was anyone watching over it then?" I couldn't believe they had overlooked the intermission during yesterday's reconstruction. I had only thought of it now myself. The intermission had lasted fifteen minutes, plenty of time for someone to slip back onstage and drop something in the bottle, or even to switch bottles.

I said as much to Laura.

"We did discuss that, Dad, but by the end of the first act, Tony had spotted the tray and took it back to the prop room to chill the tea until it was time to put it back for Agnes to pick up and bring in."

That must have been part of a conversation that I hadn't heard. "That's good, then, or else the case would be wide open again."

"Yes, it is. Sorry, Dad, but your grandson is awake now and yelling for his breakfast. Talk to you later."

"Give him a kiss from his grandpa," I said.

Azalea arrived soon after that, and Ramses greeted her with great enthusiasm. He knew it wouldn't be long before the goodies would be forthcoming. After we exchanged greetings, I told Azalea about the attack on Lexi Hollinsworth. She immediately closed her eyes and began to pray aloud. I closed my eyes, too, and even Ramses stopped wiggling about. Azalea asked for mercy for Lexi and for her family and prayed that she would soon be restored whole to them. When she finished, I added my own *Amen*.

Azalea now devoted her full attention to preparing breakfast, and I sat and drank my coffee. A thought kept niggling at me, something I was contemplating when Kanesha called me. What was it? I had been looking up information on Anton's Resistance-fighter father — that was it — and something about Resistance fighters caught my attention.

I remembered now. They were all given cyanide capsules, or so the article had said, in case they were captured by the Nazis and wanted to escape the inevitable torture and death at their hands.

Antoine du Jardin had survived the war and hadn't needed his capsule. Had he used it for another purpose? Perhaps to take out one or several Nazis? Or had he kept it for a souvenir? One that he could well have passed on to his son, Anton.

I continued to think about that and its implications while I ate my breakfast. Should I try to find out whether Anton had inherited this capsule? Did he still have it? Or had he disposed of it long ago?

I wondered what would happen if I asked Anton point-blank about it? I had little doubt that he would understand the implications of the question, and he would refuse to answer. I decided I would have to approach Madame du Jardin and talk to her without Anton. She might not be so discreet and could tell me what I wanted to know. I recalled that Kanesha said there was no evidence of a divorce, and I wondered whether in French law a wife could testify against her husband.

I did not work on Tuesdays, and that

meant I was free to do as I liked. I decided I would go to the Farrington House and try to see Madame alone. I also intended to go by the bistro and find out why I hadn't heard from Helen Louise last night. I assumed it was because she was too tired when she got home, and she simply hadn't felt like calling. It had happened before, and I couldn't blame her, but I wanted to know she was okay.

Diesel accompanied me when I left the house at nine. Surely, I thought, Madame would be awake and ready to receive a visitor by this time. I considered stopping at the bistro first, since both it and the Farrington House were on the square, but curiosity drove me first to the hotel.

I inquired at the front desk of the Farrington House for Madame du Jardin. The clerk on duty called her room, and someone answered on the other end. The clerk gave her my name and said that I would like to speak to her, and asked if she would like the gentleman to come to her room. Evidently Madame agreed.

The clerk gave me the room number, and Diesel and I headed for the elevator. I hoped that Diesel would work his usual magic and help disarm Madame enough that she would answer my questions without thinking much about their import.

Madame met me at the already open door. "Oh, the kind Mr. 'Arris. How fortunate you come, even before I call you. And you bring the wonderful *chat* with you. Diesel, *mon amour,* say hello to your *tante Delphine.*" Diesel meowed loudly and followed closely as Madame led us into the living room of her small suite.

She gestured for me to find a place to sit. She took the small sofa, and Diesel climbed onto it with her. Madame stroked his head and cooed in French to him, and I waited for a moment before I spoke.

"You were going to call me, Madame, I think you said."

"Yes, I was," she replied. "It is this silly Anton. I am so worried about him."

My ears pricked at this statement. "Really? Is something wrong?"

"Yes, he was gone last night, and he has not come back. I am most annoyed with him."

THIRTY-THREE

"You mean he's been gone all night?" I asked, taken aback. She nodded. "When did you first realize he was missing?"

"I looked for him at nine o'clock because I wanted him to find me something," she said. "I went to his room, and he was not there. I checked again, and again, until nearly midnight, and never was he there. He is not there this morning, either."

"Did you think about calling the sheriff's office?" I asked.

"Why would I do that?" Madame asked. Her lip curled. "I know where he is, the *connard*. He is with that girl he has been chatting with since the first rehearsal. He has a sickness, I think. Young women and men. He cannot leave them alone, and when he finds one who listens to him, he becomes obsessed. He left me all alone to be with her all night. Pig." She practically spit the last word.

"Which girl are you talking about?" I asked.

"Oh, that one, you know." She waved a hand. "She have a head like helmet, you know." She made a spinning gesture over her head. "So much hair she has, and that Anton, he likes blondes."

"Is this girl's name Lexi?" I asked. The description fit, but I wanted to be sure.

Madame nodded as she caressed Diesel's head. "Yes, that is the one. He tells me she talks to him when she is not needed to do whatever she does for the play. He talks about his famous father, you know, a lot, and some young people are very impressed by that."

"Anton's father was a hero of the Resistance, wasn't he?"

Madame shrugged. "So he has said. Me, I do not know. Everyone in France says he has a father or a mother or a cousin who was a noble Resistance fighter."

"In this case, Anton is telling the truth," I said. "I found articles about his father on the Internet. He was a brave man."

"For once Anton does not lie to me," Madame said, still obviously unimpressed.

I decided to try my luck. "You know, one of the interesting things I read about these Resistance fighters is that many of them had cyanide capsules with them at all times. That way, if they got captured by the Nazis, they could kill themselves before they could be tortured and executed."

"Oh, yes, this I know. Anton, he has one of these. He said it was his father's, and he keeps it as if it is made of gold. He is not brave himself, and I do not understand why he keeps this thing."

"Have you seen it recently?" I asked, trying not to sound too eager.

"I have no interest in this thing," she said, "but I know Anton wanted to show it to this Lexi, so he took it to the theater to let her see it. I have not heard him talk about it since."

A frightening picture had begun to take shape in my mind. I decided I had to tell Madame what had happened to Lexi.

"Madame, something terrible has happened," I said. "That girl, Lexi, was the victim of a brutal attack last night. She is in the hospital right now and in a coma."

Madame's eyes grew wide in shock and dawning horror. "Anton, oh, what have you done?"

"I'm afraid so, Madame, and that's why he must be found. I'm going to call the sheriff's office right now."

She nodded vigorously while I made the

call. Kanesha answered right away, and I didn't give her time to speak. "Anton du Jardin is missing. Madame hasn't seen him since nine last night. She said he has been chatting with Lexi, and get this: He had his father's cyanide capsule."

"You can tell Madame that we know where Anton is," Kanesha said.

"Where is he?" I asked before she could continue. I feared he had committed suicide after attacking Lexi.

"He's currently sitting in a cell at the police department," Kanesha replied. "He was caught about one this morning, trying to break into the performing arts building at Athena. The campus police were on patrol, and I've had a deputy keeping an eye on the place as well."

"Why did he break in?" I asked. "What was he looking for?"

"He was trying to retrieve papers he had hidden in Lombardi's dressing room," Kanesha said. "The dressing rooms have been locked ever since the murder, however, and he hasn't been able to get back inside. My men overlooked his hiding place, but this time I had Haskell search, and he's thorough. He found what Anton wanted so desperately."

"What was that?" I asked.

"I'm not ready to reveal that yet. I still have a number of things to verify." I guessed this was why she didn't mention any of this when she called this morning. She went on. "One thing I can tell you, however, is that Jared Eckworth has an unshakable alibi."

"Really? What is it?" I was suspicious.

"At the time of the attack, he was at home regaling his parents and several of their neighbors by giving them a one-man performance of the play, with him in the leading role."

I almost laughed, more out of sheer relief than anything else. With Jared out of the picture, then Anton had to be the killer. But why? It frustrated me that Kanesha knew but wasn't going to tell me until she was good and ready.

"All right, I will let Madame know where Anton is," I said.

"Tell her I will be coming to talk to her in about half an hour," Kanesha said. "And I expect you not to be there."

"Understood." I ended the call.

Madame had been listening closely to my side of the conversation. She immediately asked, "Where is the *connard*?"

"In the city jail," I told her. "The police at the college caught him trying to break into the performing arts center about one this morning. They seem to think he was after something he had hidden in the dressing room there. The police have now found it, but Deputy Berry wouldn't tell me what it was."

Madame shook her head. "The fool. I tell him he should put his important papers in the safe at the hotel, but he does not trust them, he says. So, he takes them to the theater. He is an idiot."

"Do you know what the papers are?" I almost held my breath waiting for her to respond.

"Of course I do. The idiot does not put them away, and I find them and look at them. That is why he should have put them in the safe."

"What are they?" I said, trying not to get testy with her circumlocutions.

"His insurance policies," she said in a dismissive tone. "He spends so much money on these insurances, it is ridiculous."

"Did he take out an insurance policy on Luke Lombardi?" I asked.

She shrugged. "He knows that my Luc didn't leave him anything in his will. He has known this for years, because Luc tells him so. That is why he made my Luc agree that he could have this insurance, as long as Anton himself, he pays for it."

"But, Madame," I said, "before, when you came to my house, you told Anton that he didn't get any money from Luke's will, and Anton said he did not know this?"

Madame looked away. She sighed and looked back at me. "Anton and me, we lie to you then. I am sorry. It was not a good thing to do. But Anton, he is afraid of the police, you see."

"Yes, I see." I decided to press on and come back in a moment to the possibility of Madame's complicity.

"Do you remember how much the policy is worth?" I asked.

"It is for five hundred thousand dollars," Madame said complacently. "I guess now Anton will be rich, and he will share that money with me."

"If the authorities find Anton guilty of Lombardi's murder," I said gently, "then Anton will not be able to collect on the policy. A murderer can't collect on insurance of a person he has killed."

Madame shrieked. "Of course it is this way. Anton is a fool. He was born a fool, and now he will die a fool. Why did I not see this before?" She shook her head.

The shriek had startled Diesel into jumping down and coming to sit beside me. Madame appeared not to notice.

"Did you ever tell Deputy Berry about Anton's insurance policy?" I asked.

Madame appeared not to have heard me. "That *connard.* He takes out a policy on me also. For two hundred thousand. I guess he thinks he will murder me next, and he will be rich. I could kill him, but maybe I take out insurance on him first."

I repeated my question, and Madame shrugged. "I do not like the police. I do not tell them things because then they think I am guilty, like Anton."

"Didn't you suspect that Anton was the killer?" I asked, trying to figure out how much Madame understood of the situation.

She shrugged again. "Perhaps I suspect, but I have no proof. And if Anton is going to get five hundred thousand dollars, then I want a share. I have nothing, and I cannot live on nothing."

I decided there was no point in trying to talk any further about this. The woman seemed devoid of any moral sense over the murder of her lover by her alleged ex-husband. Kanesha could handle things here. I rose.

"Madame, I must take leave of you. Deputy Berry will be here soon to talk to you," I said.

Madame looked alarmed. "You will stay

with me so I do not talk to that *femme formidable* alone."

She was right about that. Kanesha was the most formidable woman I knew, except perhaps Azalea, her mother.

"I am sorry, Madame, but I must go. Deputy Berry told me I could not stay, and as you say, she is formidable. Come on, Diesel, say goodbye to Madame."

Diesel trilled and warbled for her, and she smiled. "Goodbye, *mon amour.* You are so kind to bring him to see me, Mr. 'Arris. Thank you."

"You're most welcome, Madame, and thank you for talking to me this morning."

She waved that away, and Diesel and I took our leave. I headed straight out of the hotel and down the block to Helen Louise's bistro.

She looked up right away when we came in, and she smiled so happily that all my fears were allayed. She came out from behind the counter to hug me and give Diesel an enthusiastic rub of the head. "I've been wanting to talk to you," she said after a quick kiss. "I feel like an idiot. I dropped my phone in a sink full of hot, soapy water here last night and didn't realize it until it had been soaking for about half an hour. That killed it completely, of course. It was late when it happened, and I haven't had time to take care of replacing it yet."

"I'm sorry. That is awful. I know how I'd feel without mine. Can I do anything to help?"

"No, Debbie should be in soon for her shift, and then I can make a run to the phone store and get a replacement. Any news?"

I nodded. "I think the case is over. I believe Anton is the killer because he had taken out an insurance policy on Lombardi and wanted money."

"Unbelievable," Helen Louise said. "Didn't he realize he wouldn't be able to collect if he was found guilty?"

"He probably thought they'd never catch him. Look, I don't have all the details yet, but hopefully I'll find out more soon. When I do, we'll have dinner, and I'll tell you all about it. How's that?"

"Sounds perfect," she said, and kissed me again.

We had that dinner two nights later, only the two of us, and Diesel naturally, at her house. While we ate, I told her about my final conversation with Madame du Jardin.

Helen Louise grimaced when I finished. "The woman apparently has no con-

391

science," she said. "If she had only told Kanesha everything she knew, the case would have been solved so quickly, and Lexi wouldn't have been hurt. What is wrong with her?"

"I think she's completely self-absorbed, and she has no love for the police," I said. "She was focused on the money she would get, and it never dawned on her that Anton wouldn't be able to collect on his policy."

Next I gave her a rundown of what Kanesha had finally shared with me.

"Once Kanesha confronted him with the insurance policy and asked him about the cyanide capsule, he broke down and confessed. Kanesha had already found out through the French police that he had a record of inappropriate behavior with young men and women. Lexi Hollinsworth caught his eye. She's actually twenty-one, I think, but she looks younger. He started chatting her up and bragged about his heroic father. Apparently, that was his usual strategy. He would also let them believe he was a war hero as well. Madame filled in many of the blanks on his techniques for Kanesha."

"I guess he showed Lexi the capsule?" Helen Louise asked.

"He did, and that was the reason he attacked her later. He knew she would eventually speak up about it, and he wanted her out of the way. She is still in a coma, unfortunately, but the last Kanesha heard, she is getting stronger. She could wake up anytime now, so the doctors and her family are all really hopeful."

"That poor girl. I'll certainly be praying for her," Helen Louise said. "Anton is simply evil and completely cold-blooded."

"I'm not going to argue with you. I could wring his neck because he put Laura in such danger," I said with some heat.

"Don't blame you," Helen Louise said. "When did he manage to get the cyanide capsule in the bottle?"

"He lied about going to the bathroom during the first act. Both times he said he went to the bathroom, he was actually trying to get to the bottle and drop the capsule in. The first time Agnes frustrated him. Lexi had left to do something, and Agnes was standing by. The second time, he got lucky. Both girls were there, but they were facing away from the tray and the bottles. He popped the capsule in and went back to where he had been in the wings before Jared returned from the bathroom. If anyone had asked him, Anton would have said he had used the bathroom in Lombardi's dressing room, not the common one that everyone else used."

"What I don't understand is why he suddenly felt the need so badly for the money," Helen Louise said. "Why did he kill Lombardi now?"

"According to Madame, Anton knew Lombardi hadn't included him in his will. That was why he agreed to let Anton take out a life insurance policy on him, which frankly was stupid, as long as Anton paid the premiums and didn't expect him to. I think Anton finally had enough of the abusive treatment he received from Lombardi and decided to kill him and get the money."

Helen Louise shook her head. " 'Lord, what fools these mortals be!' "

I laughed. "You quoted Shakespeare."

"I quoted *A Midsummer Night's Dream,* to be exact." Helen Louise grinned.

"Laura is rubbing off on both of us," I said as I recalled my recent quotations to my daughter.

"Even though I'm a lawyer and a chef," Helen Louise said, "I have my literary side, too."

"I love all your sides." I raised my glass to her, and she lifted hers in response. I had learned a quote from Lord Byron just for tonight. I quoted:

She walks in beauty, like the night
Of cloudless climes and starry skies;
And all that's best of dark and bright
Meet in her aspect and her eyes;
Thus mellowed to that tender light
Which heaven to gaudy day denies.

Helen Louise had teared up, but she smiled happily. "Thank you, love. That was so sweet. I love you, Charlie Harris."

I stared at her for a long moment. The time seemed right. I had thought so much about this moment. I knew my late wife, Jackie, would approve. I looked across the table at Helen Louise, putting as much love into my expression as I could.

"Helen Louise Brady, will you marry me and make me the happiest man on earth?" Corny, I knew, but I meant every syllable.

Helen Louise's eyes sparkled. "I will marry you, Charlie Harris, but only if Diesel thinks it's a good idea."

Thus called upon, Diesel meowed loudly and enthusiastically.

ABOUT THE AUTHOR

Miranda James is the *New York Times* bestselling author of the Cat in the Stacks Mysteries, including *The Pawful Truth, Six Cats a Slayin'*, and *Claws for Concern*, as well as the Southern Ladies Mysteries, including *Fixing to Die, Digging Up the Dirt*, and *Dead with the Wind.* James lives in Mississippi.

The employees of Thorndike Press hope you have enjoyed this Large Print book. All our Thorndike, Wheeler, and Kennebec Large Print titles are designed for easy reading, and all our books are made to last. Other Thorndike Press Large Print books are available at your library, through selected bookstores, or directly from us.

For information about titles, please call:
(800) 223-1244

or visit our website at:
gale.com/thorndike

To share your comments, please write:
Publisher
Thorndike Press
10 Water St., Suite 310
Waterville, ME 04901

CPSIA information can be obtained
at www.ICGtesting.com
Printed in the USA
BVHW032158231120
594071BV00001B/14